HOW TO DO THE INNER WORK

A Guide to Self-Discovery, Empowerment, and Emotional Healing

SUSANNE MADSEN

TCK PUBLISHING.COM

Table of Contents

Introduction 1

    Happiness Is an Inside Job 4

Chapter 1: Listening to Your Inner Wisdom 9

    Why Do We Behave the Way We Do? 12

    Cultivating Appreciation and Self-Compassion..................... 15

    Your Inner Critic... 17

    Find Your Safe and Happy Place Exercise............................. 19

    Listen to Your Inner Wisdom Exercise 20

    Appreciating Yourself Exercise.. 22

    Feeling All of Your Strengths Exercise.................................. 23

Chapter 2: Restoring Your Energy Levels 24

    Free Up Time to Connect Authentically With Yourself 26

    Reducing Your Energy Drainers Exercise 29

    Why You Sometimes Ignore Your Fundamental Needs 30

    Becoming Aware of Your Limiting Beliefs Exercise 35

    Expressing Your Boundaries to Others 36

    Dealing With Controlling or Aggressive Behavior 39

    Expressing Your Boundaries to Others Exercise 43

Chapter 3: Living by Your Core Values...................................45

    Doing More of What You Truly Love 46

    Identify a Rejuvenating Activity Exercise 49

    Identify Your Deepest Held Needs and Values 50

    What Makes Your Heart Sing Exercise................................. 55

    Be the Change You Wish to See in the World...................... 56

    Allow Yourself to Dream... 59

    Identify Your Higher Purpose Exercise 62

The Power of Passion Circles 64

The Passion Circles Exercise 68

Who Are You When You're at Your Best? 69

Your Inner Resources 72

Identify Your Inner Resources Exercise 75

Chapter 4: Using Your Breath to Come Home to Yourself 76

Embrace the Challenge of Sitting Still Exercise 80

Becoming More Conscious of Your Breath 81

Breathing Through Your Limitations Exercise 83

How the Breath Affects Your Nervous System 84

Stimulating the Parasympathetic Nervous System 87

Breathing to Decrease Your Stress Exercise 89

Coherent Breathing 90

Coherent Breathing Exercise 91

Alternate Nostril Breathing 92

Alternate Nostril Breathing Exercise 94

Holotropic Breathwork 95

Chapter 5: Using Meditation to Connect to the Peacefulness of

Your Heart 98

Being in the Present Moment Exercise 102

The Benefits of Meditation 103

Connecting to Your Heart 107

Connecting to Your Heart Exercise 108

The Science of the Heart 110

Practicing Gratitude 112

Powerful Stories 114

Appreciation and Gratefulness Exercise 117

Emotional Blockages 118

Loving-Kindness Meditation 120

Loving-Kindness Meditation Exercise 122

Chapter 6: Befriending Your Challenging Thoughts and Emotions **125**

    How to Release Emotions.................................... 127

    Somatic Experiencing 132

    Working Through Challenging Emotions Exercise............. 134

    Emotional Freedom Technique............................. 136

    Expressive Writing.. 139

    Expressive Writing Exercise................................. 141

    Embracing Emotions as They Appear................... 141

    Dealing With Fear and Worry.............................. 144

    Shining the Light on Your Limiting Beliefs 146

    Change Your Story Exercise................................. 151

    Change Your Expectations for Appreciation......... 153

References **156**

Acknowledgements **158**

Introduction

"Peace does not mean to be in a place where there is no noise, trouble, or hard work. It means to be in the midst of those things and still be calm in your heart."
—Unknown.

I experienced one of the biggest light-bulb moments of my life during my first session with a leadership coach. A switch was flicked inside of me, giving me access to a greater level of awareness and empowerment. That day changed my life forever.

I came to the coaching session thinking *Help! I'm exhausted. I work too much and I'm always stressed. What should I do?* Within an hour, I clearly saw how it was my own level of thinking that was holding me back. I realized that no one was putting pressure on me and no one was stopping me from leaving the office at 6pm. The key to my happiness was in my own hands. My compulsion to work hard was a result of my internal thoughts and beliefs, and I had the power to change them.

I had been chasing ever-larger and more prestigious business projects for over a decade, and I was exhausted. After several years of putting my work ahead of my need for rest, recovery, and purpose, I felt drained and unfulfilled. I had been working way too much and my habits and thinking patterns caused me to feel intense pressure on a daily basis. I wanted to be the perfect manager who didn't let anyone else down no matter what. But when I was so busy trying not to let anyone else down, I let myself down. I suffered from IBS, had difficulty sleeping, and my foot was inflamed so badly I could barely walk.

Pouring my energy into my professional career seemed like the perfect escape from the discomfort of my emotions. In my job I got to be strong, make decisions, have fun, and receive validation. When I was busy with work, there was little need for introspection and feeling my emotions. My career had become my protective shield that I could use to avoid feeling sad, restless, sensitive, and vulnerable.

Growing up, I never learned how to observe and accept my emotions. As it turned out, no one else in my family knew how to understand and manage their emotions either—or how to truly understand the emotions of others. When I expressed my intense feelings of anger, sadness, doubt, or frustration, my emotions were often minimized or dismissed. I remember being told that I was much prettier with a smile on my face, and the day I came back from school overjoyed because I got all A's I was told to "calm down, don't think you're so special." I was hurting from these scars for decades, but I couldn't see them until I did the deep work of healing.

Many of us experience everyday situations as children where we don't feel safe or free to express our emotions. For some, these experiences create scars in our hearts and minds. Even if we haven't experienced a major traumatic event, we can still become wounded and distressed as a result of not feeling seen, accepted, and understood. In fact, most of us have emotional scars from our formative years that affect us well into adult life.

I went on to develop an eating disorder as a teenager which stayed with me for years. My mom realized what was happening, but none of us knew how to talk about it, so we didn't. I was silently screaming inside, but instead of getting the help I needed, I got better at hiding the problem. What should have been a reason to band together and get help instead reinforced how much we were unable to process and talk about our emotions.

I learned that it was safer if I ignored my emotions, put a positive spin on things, and didn't let people see how I really felt. My suppressed emotions were bubbling over and I was unsure what to do with the pent-up energy. Eventually I concluded that I needed to channel my emotions into something constructive. That's when I began my decades-long attempt to prove my worth to the world through my career.

Eighteen years later, I could no longer ignore the stress-signals I was getting from my body. I realized I had to slow down and get back in touch with the deeper and more authentic parts of myself. I longed for my life to have more meaning and I desperately wanted to feel calmer and less stressed.

That light-bulb moment in my first coaching session gave me the clarity I needed. I had woken up and I felt deeply touched and inspired by the experience. I clearly saw that we have the power within us to radically transform our lives and that life isn't about being a victim of what happens *to* us. It's about how we think, feel, and respond to what happens.

My passion was sparked and I soon enrolled in a year-long program to become a coach myself. I wasn't sure where it would lead me or how coaching would fit into my life. I just knew I had to explore it and experience more of it for myself.

I had felt stuck for so long and coaching got me unstuck. I dove head-first into this new world of self-discovery and empowerment. A world of exploring and questioning the many beliefs I had. And a world of service and helping others find their path. I was fascinated by what I learned and I was frequently moved to tears by the effect it had on the people with whom I practiced. I saw how it's possible to transform our lives when we get clear on what's important to us, why it's important, and what's holding us back. When we bring to light the darkness inside that has been sabotaging us, we can, with great care and compassion, begin to heal.

Applying the coaching techniques to my own life, I began to carve out a new path for myself as an author, speaker, and leadership coach. I had followed my passion and injected new meaning into my life. Everything fell into place. I was making a difference and I loved what I did. I was traveling the world running workshops and published two business books. But even though I had created a deeply fulfilling career and woke up most mornings feeling inspired and full of energy, I still had more work to do at an emotional level.

My state of mind and emotional wellbeing were too dependent on what was going on in my external environment. I overreacted in certain situations where others might just shrug their shoulders, and I often felt like my internal world was still out of control. I noticed that when things worked out as planned, I would feel happy and content. When they didn't, I would feel stressed and angry. And sometimes I'd feel embarrassed about my reactions because I thought I shouldn't be that upset about such a small thing. There I was again, resisting my feelings.

I wanted to change the way I reacted to external events so I could experience more peace, joy, and meaning. More so, I knew it was possible. Slowly but surely, by using the tools and methods I will share with you in this book, I made incredible progress. Therapy, breathwork, mindfulness, coaching, and several mind-body modalities helped me change my thought patterns and strengthen my ability to accept difficult emotions within myself. As a result, I became more centered and was better able to navigate the emotions, thoughts, and experiences that used to ruin my day.

Happiness Is an Inside Job

When I realized that my soul was calling for more meaningful work, and when I finally listened to and acted on my inner messages, my body and mind began to heal. You might think the solution was for me to just change my career, but I know through experience that changing external circumstances isn't enough. Joy, fulfillment, and inner peace isn't determined by what happens outside of us. What happens on the inside and how our brain processes our external reality determines our inner experiences.[1]

Yes, we do have to change our behavior in the outer world to get different results. But if all we do is focus on changing the outer world without addressing what's going on inside, we'll continue to feel anxious, stuck, and unfulfilled. We have to learn to manage our internal world while figuring out how to best respond to our external circumstances.

It's easy to get fooled into thinking that the answer to our problems lie outside of us. If only I could land my dream job and get the recognition that I long for, then I'd be happy. If only my partner would change and stop arguing with me, then my problems would melt away. If only the right politician would get elected, then I'd feel confident about the future. But looking for the answer on the outside doesn't address the root of our problems. In fact, it often leaves us wanting more. We become addicted to the wanting and yearning and controlling. When we focus too much on the outer world while ignoring our inner world, we stay stuck, no matter how much the outer world changes.

True happiness is an inside job. The external circumstances of our life do matter, but we cannot control circumstances. No matter how hard we work, life will confront us with challenging thoughts and situations, or even illnesses, that make us feel worried, angry, sad, or hopeless. The only thing we have any real control over is our internal world: how we relate to our emotions, how we use our mind and body, and the actions we decide to take.

My goal with this book is to help you live a fulfilling and purposeful life and find peace within yourself in every way possible. You may long for your voice to be heard, or wish to find a job that better fits the life you want to live. Or perhaps you are already working in a field you love, but on the inside your emotions are nagging you—you overreact, find it hard to enjoy the present moment, and just don't feel happy. No matter your situation, you will find insights and exercises in this book that have already helped many people just like you.

In my work as an executive coach, I've witnessed too many people suffer with doubt, stress, and insecurities because they didn't have an inner toolbox that could help them. By working with our inner world—thoughts, beliefs, emotions, body, and breath—we can move beyond low self-esteem, burn-out, lack of purpose, and a general sense of unhappiness. You have the power to change your experience of yourself and your external reality so dramatically that you'll never want to go back to your old habits that have created so much unnecessary stress and struggle.

Life is about how we respond to what happens, not what happens *to* us. Can we tolerate the discomfort and emotional turmoil of challenging situations? Can we sit with the fear, pain, and embarrassment of any given moment and be okay with it? Can we feel our emotions fully without turning away or trying to avoid them? Can we embrace challenging experiences with open arms and stay present?

Most of us have been taught to react unconsciously when life happens instead of responding intentionally. We send an angry email to a co-worker, blaming them for a mistake that created more work for us. We start looking for a new job because we can't handle the disappointing feedback we receive from our boss. It's easier to blame someone or run away than to sit with our feelings of sadness, anger, and rejection. We spend so much effort and energy avoiding our feelings when the best path is often to be present with our emotions and learn from them.

Unconscious reactions aren't wrong or bad. But if we can widen our perspective, we can see clearly when our reactive behavior doesn't serve us. Knee-jerk reactions keep us small and lock us into a defensive mode of relating to life and other people.

When we hastily fix or change something based on anger or fear, we often make matters worse.

My hope is that by reading this book you get to a place where you understand your emotions and can tolerate emotional discomfort. If I give you negative feedback for instance, it may bring up feelings of shame, inadequacy, anger, or guilt in you. But if you're okay experiencing these emotions, you don't have to be defensive or use any other strategy to get away from them. When you can be present with the emotions you feel in any given moment, you have true freedom to choose how to respond. Then, you may come to see the most freeing response to a sticky situation isn't to run away, nor to change someone or something outside of you, but to be still, embrace the discomfort, and find clarity inside yourself.

As you increase your emotional tolerance, you will begin to appreciate life's inevitable painful moments as opportunities to deepen your relationship with yourself. You will begin to appreciate that everything in life is there to serve you, teach you, and guide you in the right direction. With an open heart and mind, you will shine a light on the darker aspects of your personality and learn to befriend them. The discomfort may still be there, but now you can be in the discomfort and see it for what it is, just another fleeting experience of sensations and feelings in your body. That in itself will give you a profound sense of freedom and inner peace.

In this book, I will take you on a journey of developing your inner resources and changing the patterns that tend to keep you stuck and feeling overwhelmed. I like to think of this process of personal and emotional growth as a journey of homecoming. You will integrate the parts of yourself that you have abandoned or forgotten and make peace with emotions and inner experiences that you may have been fighting since a young age.

To get the most out of the book you will need to show up with a curious mind, a desire to learn something new about yourself, and the willingness to complete the short exercises that accompany each chapter. If you feel resistance to any part of the journey, that's okay. Simply notice your emotions with an open mind. You will explore many different concepts and exercises throughout this journey, and you don't have to engage with all of them at the same time. Take what works for you and leave behind what doesn't.

Throughout the book, I will speak to you as a fellow explorer and seeker, rather than a teacher who's got it all figured out (trust me, I don't!). I'm on this journey of self-discovery and healing just as much as you are. I'm on this journey with you and I want to help support you through the pain and challenges we all experience in life.

Doing the inner work and discovering who we are at our core is a life-long process. It's like the lotus flower that grows from the mud and finally blooms with all its splendor as it reaches the light above the surface of the pond. Like you, I'm on a journey of growth through the murky waters, always reaching for the light above.

Let's grow!

CHAPTER 1:

Listening to Your Inner Wisdom

"You can search throughout the entire universe for someone who is more deserving of your love and affection than you are yourself, and that person is not to be found anywhere. You, yourself, as much as anybody in the entire universe, deserve your love and affection."
—*Sharon Salzberg*

When there is alignment between the values we hold deep in our heart and how we live our life, we feel a sense of flow, joy, and purpose. It's as if something falls into place, an inner knowing, telling us that we're on the right track. We may have a surge of excitement and energy. Not a frantic, shallow energy that quickly burns out, but a strong, calm energy coming from the depth of our being.

You may recognize this empowering feeling from times in your life when you moved forward in a direction that just felt right. Perhaps when you chose what to study in school, moved to a new city, embarked on a new project, met your life partner, or decided to start a family. Your innermost values were in alignment with your outermost actions. What you thought and felt inside was reflected in what you said and did outside.

You may also feel this alignment on a smaller scale in your day-to-day life. Perhaps when you are solving an interesting problem, creating something new, engaging with your favorite sport, playing music, walking in nature, connecting with your community, caring for a loved one, engaging in spiritual practice, or when you have a meaningful conversation with a friend. In those moments you will feel a profound sense of joy and satisfaction because you are expressing and living the values that are most important to you.

When there is lack of alignment, you feel that too. You intuitively know that something isn't quite right even if you try to ignore it or force yourself to forget about it and move on. Perhaps you're in the wrong job, the wrong relationship, or the wrong city. Misalignment can also show up in everyday situations, such as having a discussion and holding back what you really think, or feeling an urge to spend more time with a loved one but ignoring it.

When you're out of alignment you intuitively know that something is missing from your life. You might not know how to describe that feeling, but if you sit still long enough and pay attention, you will feel like something is off. If you cultivate enough awareness, you will figure out what is off and you'll know what to do about it—or at least the next step to take in the right direction.

Another example of misalignment is when you neglect yourself by not spending enough time on what is most important to you. Maybe you work too many hours, give too much to others, and are not spending enough time taking care of your own health and wellbeing. If you neglect yourself long enough, you will feel unhappy and exhausted. When you don't honor your values and meet some of your essential needs for long enough, burnout, depression, or feelings of being overwhelmed will likely be the result. In addition, feelings of guilt or obligation may arise and hold you back from taking time out for yourself and doing the things that bring you joy.

Whenever you feel exhausted, unhappy, stuck, or like something is wrong, it's because you're somehow not in alignment. It means that there is some kind of disharmony between what you think and feel on the inside and what you say and do on the outside. If you recognize that sinking feeling of something not quite lining up, don't despair. This is feedback from your internal guidance system helping you get your life back in alignment with your values and needs.

Coming into alignment is a gradual process that takes time. As we move through life, we come to understand who we are, what we value, what our strengths are, and what we will and will not accept. We grow and learn and we get feedback from our senses about what works for us and what doesn't. The trick is to listen to your intuition—that inner knowing, inner voice, or inner feeling—and take the feedback seriously.

Unfortunately, many of us don't act on the signals we get from within because we're too caught up in chasing something that's not authentic to us. We're trying to please someone else, gain acceptance from someone else, or chase a career or a lifestyle we think we need.

Caroline Myss, who has authored ten books about wellness and mysticism, says that everyone has access to intuitive guidance all the time.[2] The problem is that we often dismiss the subtle hints we get from within because, if we really paid attention long enough, we would intensely feel that misalignment. And those feelings of shame, guilt, fear, and frustration can be scary and overwhelming. Truly trusting our intuition requires us to get up and make a change. It may seem easier to just avoid those feelings and keep things the same. But what's the worst that can happen if you listen and act on your inner wisdom? And what's the worst that can happen if you don't?

Taking radical action can be uncomfortable. Perhaps you're afraid of saying no and disappointing others, or you have lost the belief in your own ability to learn and grow and achieve something new or different. Perhaps you have abandoned yourself and given your power away by blaming people or circumstances or playing the victim. You may think there is something wrong with you, but it's really just your perspective that's getting in the way.

I've worked with many people who felt trapped and unhappy in their lives, wanting more peace and alignment but struggling to find it. And I've been there myself. Although a part of me enjoyed working in the financial center of London, deep in my stomach I felt that my job wasn't profoundly meaningful and that it wasn't well aligned with my strengths, interests, and values. For several years I struggled because I kept focusing on making progress at work and avoiding my feelings. The uneasy feeling in my stomach vanished when I dared to carve out a new career for myself as an independent leadership coach. As soon as I got on to the path of coaching, I felt an immense sense of purpose and joy in what I was doing. I went from feeling misaligned in my work to aligned because my inner world of dreams, desires, and creativity was now in sync with my outer world and how I spent my time each day.

As a coach I work with people who feel stuck and victimized by past events and who aren't putting their strengths and talents to full use. Many of the business executives I work with struggle with low self-esteem and have difficulties setting boundaries. But no matter where you come from or where you are now, I want you to know that you are capable of making adjustments to your life that change how you think and feel about yourself. Not only have I made big shifts in my own life, I've also witnessed major changes in so many clients that I've worked with. If you feel misaligned, stuck, or unsure, that's okay because I'm about to help you find more clarity. First, you have to ask yourself an important question: why?

Why Do We Behave the Way We Do?

Let's explore where our beliefs come from and why we behave the way we do.

As young children we don't have the capacity to think rationally about our surroundings and why our parents, teachers, or classmates act the way they do. All we experience is our interpretation to their actions—feeling fully loved, cared for, and accepted, or feeling shamed, excluded, unseen, unheard, or disrespected. When our basic need for love, acceptance, and safety isn't met in certain situations, our survival instinct kicks in. We begin to find strategies that help us feel safe and get the love and acceptance we need.

For example, when your sister makes fun of you for how you look, or repeatedly tells you that you're not clever enough to work things out, you begin to believe that you really are less worthy and not as smart as other kids. To protect yourself from the embarrassment, you begin to withdraw from social situations and stay quiet instead of speaking up when you have an idea you want to share. While this strategy makes you feel accepted by your sister, it's easy to see how it will have a negative impact on many other parts of your life.

When our basic need for love, acceptance, and safety isn't met, we may become protective, manipulative, aggressive, people-pleasing, or self-blaming. In other words, we begin to adopt coping strategies and abandon our true selves. We close our hearts, we disown the parts of us that are not accepted, and we create certain stories and beliefs, that help us survive and make sense of our reality. In other words, we create a mental model of ourselves and of our surroundings, and a unique lens through which we view the word, which is based on our experiences.

Our brain is constantly trying to make sense of the world in order to keep us safe, so everything we experience gets stored in our brain's mental model. We can compare it to a set of software programs that get installed onto a hard drive, enabling us to make use of the computer. A child without any programming cannot function in the world, so our brains automatically start writing programs to teach us how to stay safe and adapt to the world we're living in. When you get bullied for crying at school, you learn not to cry or express sadness or hurt in front of others.

This program may work to save you from the embarrassment at school of being bullied, but it won't help you in your marriage or with your children. If you want to change a computer program, you just click a button. But changing your own subconscious programs from when you were a child takes a lot more knowledge and skill.

Bruce Lipton, the bestselling author of *The Biology of Belief*, explains that between the ages of two and six, our brainwaves are mostly in the Theta frequency range.[3] Theta brainwaves are associated with imagination and hypnosis, which enables us to download and install subconscious programs more easily. In this "super learning state," our brains are open to suggestions from our caretakers and likely to accept what we're told, just like you would be if hypnotized into a Theta state. As teenagers and adults, our brainwaves mostly operate in Beta. In a Beta state, the brain is better able to focus and think analytically. It's not a state which helps us to easily take on a new belief system.

What this means, is that you can't just click a button to remove your limiting beliefs and download a completely new operating model. But with conscious effort, curiosity, and a healthy dose of self-compassion, it *is* possible to become aware of your patterns, and to change them. You can begin to change your unwanted programming by practicing awareness and self-inquiry, and I'll show you how to do that at the end of this chapter.

When we become aware of the beliefs we hold about ourselves and the world, we begin to understand why we behave the way we do. We begin to see why we have issues in our relationships, in our careers, with our finances, and with our health. Coming into awareness is not about placing blame on others or finding faults with our current way of thinking. It is simply about creating a greater understanding of our programming so that we can change it. If we want to live with more purpose, joy, and ease, we have to get to the root of why we're so hard on ourselves and why we're not doing what we know is best for us.

Cultivating Appreciation and Self-Compassion

What happens the day you wake up and are brave enough to admit that you have strayed too far from your center? What happens when you can no longer ignore the part of you that feels deeply unhappy? What do you do when you feel trapped and exhausted? And what do you do if you fear the consequences of making the adjustments you secretly dream of?

The most important thing you can do is to stop and pause. Find a moment of stillness and take some slow, deep breaths. Instead of covering up your feelings or running away from the issues that nag you, give yourself permission to feel what needs to be felt and to connect with the innermost part of you—the part that intuitively knows what is right for you and what you truly long for. You can call it your inner wisdom, internal guidance system, higher self, intuitive intelligence, center, or whatever resonates with you.

Being still and listening to the subtle signs within you isn't particularly easy, but it is simple. Just be still and listen to that wise guru inside. When you sit still and listen, you will realize that you almost always know what you need. You have the answers and the medicine inside. You may even realize that all you ever needed is already here, hidden in the stillness, and that you don't want to go back to running around like you did before.

To connect with the wise part of your being, you will have to be curious, open, and relaxed. You can't listen to your inner wisdom when you're stressed out and constantly worry about the future. You have to create space to listen to yourself.

As you open up and listen inwards, you may initially feel sad and vulnerable because you're admitting that things aren't the way you would like them to be. That's perfectly normal and okay. It can hurt to acknowledge the truth.

No matter what comes up for you, it's important that you support yourself with kindness, appreciation, and self-compassion. Appreciation is about acknowledging the good things about you and really feeling them in your heart. It's not an arrogant or egotistical act. You're not telling yourself that you're better than others. Self-compassion is being gentle with yourself when confronted with limiting beliefs and painful thoughts and emotions. When you support yourself emotionally by bringing compassion to your vulnerability and emotional pain, you will be better able to feel what needs to be felt and to engage in positive change.

Kristin Neff has written extensively about self-compassion. She says that instead of replacing negative feelings with positive ones, self-compassion is about generating new positive emotions by embracing the negative ones. When we have compassion for ourselves, she writes, the positive emotions of care and connectedness are felt alongside our painful feelings. According to Neff, this is important, because it ensures that the fuel of resistance isn't added to the fire of negativity. The more you resist your negative emotions, the more turmoil you will find inside of you. It can seem counterintuitive, but embracing your negative emotions creates a positive experience. Self-compassion along with introspection allows us to celebrate the entire range of human experience, so that we can become whole and transcend our outdated programming.[4]

Some people mistakenly believe that if they're too kind to themselves they'll become complacent and won't take action to improve their situation. But research shows that nothing could be further from the truth. Instead of evading personal accountability, self-compassion actually strengthens it. Not only is self-compassion a powerful way to increase your motivation, it also makes a big difference in your ability to survive and thrive when you go through difficult experiences.[5]

Unfortunately, many people struggle to show love and compassion for themselves, let alone acknowledge their talents and achievements. Even the most successful executives experience this sometimes. I recently coached a director from a large firm. Joe (not his real name) was due to attend a training program with twenty other executives he had never met before. He was apprehensive and nervous at the thought that he might be dwarfed by the other executives. He was worried that they would be smarter than him and more senior, even though he was a director.

I asked Joe to imagine that he was standing at the top of a mountain filled with his personal strengths, attributes, experiences, and knowledge. I invited him to *really feel* the size of his mountain below him and to acknowledge all of the skills and achievements he had accumulated throughout his career. One by one we listed his strengths and then Joe was asked to acknowledge that strength by feeling it in the core of his being. Finally, the penny dropped. He understood that we can never really see our own mountain because we're standing on it. We can only see how impressive other people's mountains are.

Your Inner Critic

Sadly, it's very common to have an underdeveloped appreciation for ourselves and an overdeveloped inner critic. It's part of our negative programming, which stems from being exposed to criticism, rejection, and negative messages from the media and people we spend time with. As a result, we learn to practice negative self-talk as children, and have a tendency to minimize ourselves long into adulthood. If you give someone a compliment, most people will brush it aside, not believing they deserve the attention because they feel that praising themselves is self-indulgent.

Belittling ourselves is an easy trap to fall into. We've become so accustomed to these subtle negative messages from within that they have become an integral part of who we are. That's why we need to spend time examining what that voice in our head is really saying. If we listen to our negative self-talk and believe it, it can hold us back and keep us stuck. Your negative programming may be the single biggest thing that prevents you from feeling at peace and living the authentic life you dream of.

Self-care is an essential element in coming home to yourself and interacting in loving ways with people around you. The relationship you have with yourself is a foundation for the relationships you have with others. As the crew always tells you before taking off in a plane: in the event that the oxygen masks are released, put the mask on yourself before helping anyone else. You really do need to love and care for yourself before you can appropriately love and care for anyone else. To quote Heidi Hanna, author of *The Sharp Solution*, "Taking care of ourselves isn't selfish, as the energy we bring has a direct impact on everyone around us. By recharging ourselves we are able to truly serve the people that we cross paths with."[6]

To strengthen your relationship with your own self, think about giving yourself the kind of support that you would give a child or a good friend. Imagine your best friend telling you there's an area in their life that they're not happy with. They wish things were different. Perhaps they want to lose weight, get away from a draining job, or finally do something about their mental health. How would you respond? What would you say and what would you do? Presumably, you wouldn't start shaming them or criticizing them. You would show understanding and compassion. You would tell them that it's okay. That they did the best they could with the resources they had available. You would tell them that they are not alone in feeling this way, that you'll support them in making a change, and that they can do it.

This is how you need to speak to yourself—with compassion, hope, and conviction. You *are* good enough and you have all the resources you need to make a change. You have come so far and you have worked so hard. You are standing on a mountain full of strengths, skills, and experiences. You just can't see it very well because you're standing on it. But if you close your eyes and pay attention, you can begin to feel it under your feet.

You can sense the vastness of your mountain and you can be certain that somewhere inside of it there is gold. All of your past choices, experiences, and hard work has gone into the creation of this mountain. And all of it has served you even if you're not where you would like to be in this moment in time. Trust that there is a blessing hidden in everything and that you are on this path for a reason.

It's time to put your inner critic aside and thank yourself from the bottom of your heart. Thank yourself for all the effort you have put in, for the things you have achieved, and for everything you have given. Simply thank yourself for being who you are. You *are* enough and you are beautifully unique just the way you are. Sure, you have flaws like everyone else. That's normal. No matter where you come from or what you've gone through, you are still worthy and beautiful in all your imperfection.

Find Your Safe and Happy Place Exercise

It's time for your first exercise on your journey of growth and self-discovery. It's a foundational exercise that will only take a few minutes and set you up for all the other exercises to come.

The purpose of this exercise is to identify a place where you feel totally safe and comfortable so you can reflect, feel your emotions, and intentionally work on your personal growth. By allowing yourself to visit this special place—physically and mentally—you will feel calm and centered. You will also be in a great position to practice awareness and self-inquiry and engage in the exercises that follow.

Step 1: Find a comfortable place in or around your home where you feel totally safe and at ease. Choose a place where you will not be interrupted and where your creativity can flow freely. You may want to be surrounded by something green and soothing, or whatever makes you feel safe, calm, and inspired.

Step 2: If you are not able to identify a physical place right now, then it's perfectly fine to choose a place in your imagination. To do that, simply imagine a place where you feel totally safe and at ease. A place where you feel understood, loved, and appreciated. This could be snuggled up on the sofa with your favorite music playing and a warm glow from the fire. It could be going for a walk in the countryside with your best buddy or perhaps lying on the beach in the sunshine, listening to the waves lapping the shore. Take a moment to choose a perfectly safe and rejuvenating place in your imagination right now.

Step 3: When you are ready, settle into your chosen place and close your eyes. Take three slow breaths and consciously relax your body. Breathe in through your nose and out through your mouth, letting go of any tension. Let your shoulders be loose, relax the small muscles in your face, and let your jaw drop.

Step 4: As you sit and breathe, practice giving yourself permission to slow down and to simply relax in this happy place. Tell yourself that it's okay to step away from your busy mind chatter and to-do list to create a moment of stillness. You don't have to be perfect at this. You're simply practicing letting go of doing activities so you can relax.

How was this exercise for you? Was it easy or difficult to identify a safe and happy place and to feel comfortable spending time there?

Listen to Your Inner Wisdom Exercise

The next exercise is an opportunity to connect inwards and get in touch with your intuitive guidance system. Doing the inner work is about connecting to the deeper parts of your being that you may have forgotten or pushed aside. When you connect with your inner wisdom you bypass your rational mind and get answers from deep within your being. For this exercise, and many of the following ones, you will need a pen and paper.

This exercise takes five to ten minutes, but feel free to work on it longer if you want. To access the audio-version of this exercise, go to www.susannemadsen.co.uk/inner-work.html

Step 1: Make yourself comfortable in your happy place. Close your eyes and take a few slow, relaxing breaths. Notice how the air moves in through your nostrils, down through your chest, expanding your stomach, and back out again. Simply notice the subtle sensations in your body as the air moves through you. With each exhalation, see if you can let go of tension and become a little more relaxed.

Step 2: When you are totally relaxed, ask your inner guidance system what you want more of in your life. Don't try to get it right. Simply notice the first words and images that come into your awareness and write them down. What do you want more of? Don't filter anything out. Just write whatever comes up.

Step 3: Now ask yourself what you want less of in your life. Resist the urge to filter anything out. Just write down the first intuitions that come to you without rationalizing it.

Step 4: Look back over your list. What do you notice when you look at it? Does anything surprise you?

In the chapters and exercises that follow, we will spend much more time on self-inquiry and exploring your heart's desires. What's important right now is that you have taken the first step. You've started the journey of paying attention and listening to yourself.

Appreciating Yourself Exercise

The purpose of this exercise is to help you feel deep appreciation in your heart for yourself and your journey up until now. When you feel appreciation in your heart, you will feel calm and peaceful, and you will notice a warm sensation in your entire body. Your nervous system will be regulated, your mind will be quieter, and you will be able to make better decisions. Filling your heart with gratitude will give you inner strength for the journey ahead.

Take five minutes right now to show genuine love and appreciation for yourself. Choose at least three of the options below and notice what happens in your body. Don't just think about it, feel it.

- Sit quietly with your eyes closed whispering to yourself, *Thank you. I love you.*
- Wrap your arms around your chest and give yourself a heartfelt hug.
- Perform a little dance of gratitude.
- Visualize yourself from the outside and say something nice to this person that would make them feel loved.
- Visualize a big yellow flower in the middle of your chest gradually opening up as you send yourself feelings of love and gratitude. The more you shower yourself with honest appreciation, the more the flower opens up.
- Take a gentle breath of appreciation into your chest and see if you can feel the warm sensations in your heart.
- Write yourself a love note and read it to yourself out loud.

Use your imagination and create a warm feeling of appreciation in your body. If you have trouble getting yourself to feel these feelings, that's okay. Keep practicing and you will get better at it. The more you practice, the more warmth you will feel in your heart.

Feeling All of Your Strengths Exercise

In this exercise, I invite you to go a step further by highlighting all your strengths and taking full ownership for them in your heart. The goal is to help you put your inner critic aside and continue to build your inner strength. The more you love and acknowledge yourself, the less you will be dependent on validation from sources outside of you.

Step 1: Sit quietly and take slow, deep breaths until you feel calm and relaxed.

Step 2: Bring to mind a positive attribute or strength of yours. Write it down. If you can't think of a strength, imagine what your best friend would highlight as something you're really good at.

Step 3: Take full ownership for that strength by putting it into your heart and really feeling it. You'll know it's in your heart when you feel a warm glow or a tingling sensation in your chest or abdomen. Don't rush this exercise. Give yourself the gift of opening up your heart and accepting all of your strengths and attributes.

Step 4: Identify at least five more strengths and feel the warmth of each one inside of you. That's the idea of this exercise—to feel the warmth of love and self-appreciation in your body, rather than just thinking about it.

Step 5: Now imagine you are standing on your personal mountain, filled with your strengths, attributes, and experiences. Close your eyes, relax your body, and really *feel* it below your feet. Every day, as you learn new skills and become a wiser version of yourself, the size of your mountain will grow.

CHAPTER 2:

Restoring Your Energy Levels

"Perhaps the biggest tragedy of our lives is that freedom is possible,
yet we can pass our years trapped in the same old patterns."
—*Tara Brach*

Think of yourself as having a tank of fuel. Each morning when you wake up you have a certain amount of physical, mental, and emotional energy in your tank. If you've had a bad night's sleep you may have a bit less. As you go through the day you use some of that energy, and you also add some back to the tank from activities that inspire you. Looking at your energy level from week to week, or from month to month, you want it to be fairly stable and reasonably high. That's possible when you prioritize your deepest held needs and invest time in activities that bring you joy and make you feel good. If you consistently use more energy than you generate, your tank will begin to run empty and you will feel tired and unhappy.

To feel more energized and to come back to your center, you will have to substitute the activities that drain you for activities that bring you joy and fulfillment. That sounds easy in principle, yet many of us don't do it. You may have family obligations and financial commitments that hold you back or maybe you feel constrained by self-limiting beliefs and bad habits.

In this chapter we will help you identify the activities and thought patterns that drain you so that you can set healthy boundaries and restore your energy levels. It may feel uncomfortable to examine the aspects that aren't serving you, but it's a necessary part of doing the inner work. When you eliminate some of your energy drainers and set boundaries, you will immediately feel better and free up energy for the journey ahead. In a later chapter, we will brainstorm activities that *give* you energy by identifying your deeply held values and learning how to honor them.

There will always be some things you need to do that you enjoy less than others. That's okay. It's part of life. There may be a very good reason why you're in your job right now. Perhaps it's not the most fulfilling, but it serves a higher purpose by building your skills or paying for your children's education. It could also be that you're supporting a friend or a family member who is experiencing hardship. That could be very taxing, but also purposeful and in alignment with your values. Even so, there is a limit to how much you can and should give. Remember to put the oxygen mask on yourself first. You need to keep your own energy levels up so that you are able to be there for others.

The optimal environment for personal growth and satisfaction is where you are able to balance the needs of others with the needs of yourself, and where you have enough space, time, and energy to develop and expand into a wiser version of yourself.

If there is too much stress and obligation in your life, you'll stay stuck in survival mode. That will cost you a lot of energy and can have a detrimental effect on your physical, mental, and emotional health in the long-term. In this state you will have very little energy to give to others. On the other hand, if there is too little demand on you, and too little challenge, you will feel stagnant and bored. We all need some chaos and discomfort in order to grow.

You are the only one who can determine how much chaos is healthy for you, and you are the only one who can set the necessary boundaries. If you take the time to listen to your inner guidance, you will know where in your life there is too much stress. You will know what the activities are that really drain you.

And you will know in which situations you need to say no and set better boundaries.

A great way to start analyzing the situations that drain you is to scan through all the activities you do in an average week and the people you engage with. As you do so, you consider if each activity—or person you interact with—increases your level of energy or diminishes it. The idea is simply to identify anything that zaps your energy, including activities you do out of obligation, and any self-critical or compulsory thought-patterns you engage in.

Identifying everything that drains you might make you feel low. It's not easy to admit that there is misalignment somewhere in your life. However, acknowledging the truth and listening to yourself when you feel something is off is imperative. Friends, therapists, and coaches can guide you on your journey, but you have to do the work. And the work starts with paying attention and listening to yourself.

Becoming more aware of where the biggest outflow of energy comes from gives you the option to make small adjustments that will have a positive impact. The idea is to set a few clear boundaries and to simplify some of your activities so that there is a balance between how much energy you give and how much you receive. There is no need to go overboard and start saying no to everything. Too many rules and too many changes at once will make it harder to implement. It would be much better to focus on one or two items that stand out and that will make a big difference to your daily energy levels.

Free Up Time to Connect Authentically With Yourself

Years ago, when I was working ten-hour days and commuting for two hours on top of that, I felt completely drained by the time I got home. I had little energy left for self-care or self-inquiry. I wondered how I could ever create the kind of shift I wanted. But little by little, I began to carve out time to connect more authentically with myself. I spent ten minutes in silence when I got back from work to reclaim some of my energy, and I did a short breathing exercise in the morning to center myself. I also wrote an entire page of affirmations and began reading them every morning on the train to work. None of these things took a lot of time, but they made a big difference to my wellbeing and enabled me to think more clearly about my needs and about the future I wanted to create. Instead of hoping things would get better, I took small steps to keep my mind focused on creating the life I really wanted.

Freeing up time and energy for a new level of thinking to emerge is an essential step on your journey of homecoming. Without it, you will continue in the same track—thinking the same thoughts, engaging in the same activities, and selling yourself short. If you attempt to run faster, fix more, or be more, you will add to the feeling of being overwhelmed and you'll get more of what you don't want.

By freeing up time, you create the space to take a step back and evaluate your life, how you are feeling, and what you would like to change. As you take the position of a curious onlooker, you can then begin to determine what you want more of and less of in your life. You will discover what has the most meaning to you, and what is in your way of achieving it. The ultimate goal is to bring more joy, energy, and purpose to your life. You can start by removing the things that don't serve you in order to free up time and energy for things that are more important to you.

It may feel counterintuitive to slow down and take time out for yourself when there is so much you want to do, but if you keep running, you will make matters worse and you won't be able to free up mental space for a new level of thinking to emerge. When you operate from a place of hurry, worry, or stress, your attention narrows and instead of thinking expansively and creatively, your focus will be on fighting whatever threats you feel are present in your environment.

You can start with a short daily ritual of as little as five to fifteen minutes. Spend that time sending kind thoughts to yourself, journaling, going for a mindful walk, saying a prayer, or simply sitting in stillness and observing your breath. Do whatever works for you and whatever makes you connect with that deeper and more authentic part of yourself. Like so many of the people I work with, you just might be surprised how powerful five mindful minutes can be each day.

To make space for something new to emerge, you can also make changes to your physical environment. Explore a physical location you haven't been to before or clear out your closet or garage. Clearing out and letting go of things you no longer need helps you to energetically release the old and create space for something new. Symbolically, it prepares you to release old habits and beliefs that no longer serve you.

You will also find it easier to connect with yourself and be fully present if you take a break from electronics and online activity. That means television, online news, and social media. Try to disconnect completely for half a day or perhaps for a full weekend. You will find that your focus shifts from what's going on in the world to what's happening in your immediate surroundings and within you. With that shift in focus, not only will you feel more centered, you will also be in a better position to listen to your inner guidance and understand what you might want to change going forward.

During times in my own life when I have felt low on energy and inspiration, it's often been linked to working too much and not having had a proper break for a while. I may even be so caught up in the busyness of life that I don't feel I need a break. But we all know that going away, having new experiences, soaking up the sun, and being care-free can recharge us in ways that home life cannot.

Part of the magic comes from being more outdoors, feeling connected to friends and family, having fun, and being in the present moment. Another part is switching off from work and the constant flow of meetings and emails. If you go on holiday and still check emails, you won't benefit from the vacation as much because you're keeping your mind focused on work instead of letting go. When you let go of your work and allow your mind to truly relax, you'll find it much easier to create new levels of thinking that can ultimately improve your work and the rest of your life too.

I recently went on a mindfulness retreat in a beautiful part of the country overlooking the river Dart. I thought it would be difficult to let go of work and switch off my phone for six days, but I absolutely loved it and wasn't tempted at all to switch it back on. I returned from the retreat fully present, fully charged, and with a feeling of deep inner peace. I don't think I could have experienced that if I'd been online, checking my emails.

Reducing Your Energy Drainers Exercise

The following exercise will help you restore your energy levels. I will ask you to identify all the items you find stressful and draining and then make a commitment to make a small change in a positive direction. Be prepared that it may feel uncomfortable to examine the aspects that aren't serving you. This is a necessary step on your journey of growth. So, grab hold of pen and paper and take your time as you reflect on each question. Don't rush. Set aside ten full minutes.

Step 1: Take a slow, deep breath in, and fully relax your body. Then, mentally scan through the activities of an average week as you capture your answers to the following questions:

- In which part of your life is there too much stress at the moment?
- Which situations do you find challenging and overly energy consuming?

- Which people, social media, and news feeds leave you feeling low?
- What are some of the activities you engage in out of guilt or obligation?
- Which habitual thinking patterns and self-imposed rules do you engage in that drain energy from you?

If you feel resistance to this exercise, or if it brings up negative imagery and memories, that's okay. Remember to act like your own best friend and be kind to yourself. If tears flow, let them flow. Be gentle and rest assured that you're doing the right thing. You're being honest and you're beginning to address what needs to be addressed. By reading through these pages and engaging with the exercises, you are showing that you have the guts to take an honest look at yourself and that you are ready for a new approach. That's something to be proud of.

Step 2: Now, look back over your list of items and decide on one or two actions you can take to reduce the energy drain and strengthen your boundaries.

- What activities do you need to limit or stop doing?
- What behaviors will you no longer accept from yourself or others?
- In which ways can you simplify your commitments with regards to work, household chores, significant other, family, friends, or voluntary activities?

There is no right or wrong. Simply choose one or two actions that will reduce your overall burden of stress.

Why You Sometimes Ignore Your Fundamental Needs

As you begin to listen more deeply to your inner wisdom and take full ownership of your commitments to yourself, it's worth identifying what the underlying needs are that you have been suppressing. The key here is to ponder what you really need and why you sometimes ignore these needs. For example, imagine you no longer want to stay late at work to turn around last-minute assignments from your boss. Thinking about it, it makes you resentful because you don't feel consulted in the process. You have a need to be listened to and to boost your energy levels after work with sports. Perhaps you've been ignoring your needs because of an eagerness to please and a fear of falling out of favor with your boss. Whereas this behavior may have served you in the past, perhaps it's time to make a change as it's no longer serving you.

Understanding why you have been ignoring certain needs previously can help you make a lasting change. But how do you begin to unpick the underlying reasons for your behavior? Let's say you have a pattern of wanting to please others or that you find it challenging to ask for help and admit that you don't have the bandwidth to do it all. What's the underlying reason you began to put yourself second? Why is it so challenging to talk about your needs, share your emotions and show that you're vulnerable?

A great way to gain valuable insight into your psychology is by contemplating who you had to be and what you had to do to gain the love and affection of your parents and caretakers. As children we go to great lengths to mold our behavior so that we will be accepted and taken care of. This is a rudimental part of our survival instinct. A small child is unable to survive on their own. For this reason, all children develop strategies that help them stay safe and be cared for.

The patterns you develop as a child follow you long into adult life. If your parents rewarded you for being quiet and accommodating, chances are that you still hold on to these patterns of behavior today. Likewise, if you didn't get the recognition you craved, you will likely be looking for recognition from others in your adult life. But it's not just your parents' behaviors that shaped you. If you've been shamed by a teacher, bullied by another child, or hurt by a boyfriend or girlfriend, it will likely have affected your beliefs and behaviors too.

We have all been shaped by the environment we grew up in, and it's perfectly normal that your upbringing has created limitations in the way you think and behave. The idea isn't to undo your programming but to become aware of it so you can consciously choose another way to think and behave that better serves you.

To help you identify the beliefs that prevent you from living a balanced and fulfilling life, consider sentences that begin with *I can't, I'm not good at, I must, I should,* or *I hate.* For example, *I must work hard to gain acceptance and approval.* Or *I can't ask for help because it's a sign of weakness.* Do you sometimes say to yourself that you're too much of something? For instance, *I'm too old, too young, too introverted,* or *too emotional.* Or that you're not enough—not experienced enough, not clever enough, not kind enough, not slim enough, not rich enough? These are all examples of labels and thought patterns that influence how you behave.

If you have a lot of upsetting memories and beliefs that hold you back, it can be beneficial to seek professional help from a therapist or coach. I worked with a therapist for several years and found it invaluable. My therapist helped me get in touch with the vulnerable parts of myself that I didn't want to feel and that I had conveniently tucked away. She also helped me express my deeply held needs and become more accepting of strong emotions within myself, such as anger and sadness.

Limiting thoughts and beliefs come in many shapes and sizes and can be hard to recognize because you're so used to them. The beauty is that once you become aware of your thoughts you can challenge them, change them, and learn to ignore them. You certainly don't have to be defined by them. One of the beliefs I picked up in my childhood is that being busy and productive is always good, and rest and relaxation is lazy. I don't actually think my parents meant to instill this in me quite to the extent that they did, but it doesn't take too many situations to sear a memory into a young child's mind. All I remember is being scolded on numerous occasions for relaxing and not noticing that my mom needed help in the kitchen. When I was busy with homework, I was less likely to trigger my dad's anger. This was one of the reasons I started spending more time studying.

I'm sure you can guess the impact it had on me to always prioritize being busy over and above relaxation. The upside has been my high level of productivity, but it's hard to describe the severity of the downside. Not only did I become very task-oriented, I also suffered from high levels of stress, aches and pains, and a near burnout. About ten years into my professional career, my symptoms could no longer be ignored. At the time I was working in financial services. Eager to prove myself and do a good job, I was willing to stay late most evenings to get work done. I didn't want to show vulnerability or ask for help. I wanted to compete with the big boys.

Needless to say, I was soon heading for burnout, not because the organization demanded that I work late, but because of my own programming and belief system. The enormous stress I experienced throughout my career came from myself, not the role. For sure, there were deadlines to meet, projects to deliver, and challenging conversations to be had. But I was the one that stressed myself out about it. I was the one who didn't set clear boundaries and didn't listen to my physical, mental, and emotional needs. I just kept giving more and more until I was so out of balance that my body began to protest.

In the months and years that followed I learned how important it can be to do nothing. I learned to recharge my batteries by being still and by connecting with the deeper part of my being that's not defined by what I do or by external validation.

My default is still to be active and to overachieve so I have to consciously challenge my programming and remind myself of the value of downtime.

What are some of the beliefs you adopted throughout your life, and in which ways are they influencing you today? Could it be that some of them are no longer useful and that it's time to leave them behind? Perhaps you have adopted a belief that you need to work hard to be loved and accepted, that it's weak to ask for help, that it's a failure not to be in control, or that things have to be perfect. Or perhaps you believe you are not good enough just the way you are, that you need to always be of service to others, or that you have to look good to be attractive. These beliefs can lead to disappointment, exhaustion, and a feeling of being overwhelmed if you continue to live by them.

I've seen many hard-working employees, managers, and parents put too much pressure on themselves and their surroundings without questioning the reason for their behavior. Some of the feelings of being overwhelmed are connected to what I call the superhero mentality, where we feel compelled to step in and save the day. We want things to be done to a certain standard and have difficulty trusting others to do it. As a result, we end up doing most of the work ourselves and are quick to take back control of tasks if they are not done to our standards.

There is nothing wrong with doing a good piece of work and adding value to those around us. Much transformation and purpose can come from that. But it has to be done with a high level of awareness and without playing the hero. We have to ask ourselves why we are doing what we are doing and for whose sake we are doing it. Which needs are we seeking to fulfill by being the hero? Whose toes might we be stepping on, and what is it costing us in terms of energy, frustration, and impaired relationships?

When you increase your level of awareness, you begin to understand some of the unconscious patterns that are driving you, and why you have been ignoring some of your needs while seeking to fulfill others. You may have downplayed your need for self-care at the expense of the need for acceptance and validation. Or perhaps you have ignored your need for fun and laughter and given priority to the need for control and certainty.

Understanding why you've been suppressing some of your needs is a fundamental step before you begin to express and discuss your boundaries with others. You need to take ownership for your part in the story that brought you to this place. If you're not aware of why you've been making the choices you have, you may end up blaming your employer or your spouse for why you feel tired, angry, and out of balance. In reality, you may feel drained, not because of the demands that others put on you, but because of the demands and expectations you put on yourself.

To come back to balance and find your inner home, you have to let go of your high standards and wanting to be in control. You have to release your need for external validation and instead fill up your heart from the inside. In essence, it's about giving yourself the love and recognition you crave so that you don't have to compromise and deplete yourself in order to obtain approval from external sources.

Becoming Aware of Your Limiting Beliefs Exercise

This next exercise will require some detective work on your behalf. The goal is to start making your unconscious programming more conscious. When you become more aware of your limiting beliefs, you will understand why you behave the way you do and you will find it easier to make a positive change. Set fifteen minutes aside to ponder the following questions:

- What are some of the biggest beliefs that are holding you back in your life?
- In which ways do you limit yourself by thinking; *I can't,*

I'm not good at, I must, I should, or *I hate?*

- What would you like to achieve in life but aren't currently working toward? What is your justification?
- What did you have to do as a child to keep yourself safe and gain the love and affection of your parents?
- Which fundamental needs are your limiting beliefs causing you to suppress?
- Who would you be without your limiting beliefs?

Expressing Your Boundaries to Others

As you increase your awareness about which needs are the most important to you and the boundaries you would like to set, it may be time to have a conversation with those around you.

Setting boundaries or saying no to a friend, spouse, or colleague can be challenging because you may fear you will come across as demanding or inflexible or that you will damage the relationship. With proper preparation and the right kind of approach, that's less likely to happen. A far bigger risk is that you avoid or delay the conversation and effectively keep suppressing your needs. That could fuel your resentment and allow the issue to mushroom under the surface.

Proper preparation cannot be overestimated. It helps you think through what you perceive the problem to be and what you would like to achieve from the conversation. Consider the topics you want to discuss and how you can best convey what your need is. Also reflect on how you would like your relationship with the other person to be and what kind of mindset you would like to show up with.

Then, turn the tables and reflect on how the other person might see the problem. What are *their* underlying needs and what is *their* emotional state likely to be? By considering what the other person's perspective might be, you will be more perceptive during the conversation and less likely to be caught off guard and go into defensive mode.

This kind of conversation shouldn't be about blaming the other person or about getting all of your needs met on your terms. It's about clearly articulating your concerns and your needs and discussing them in relation to the other person's concerns and needs. You each open up and negotiate your needs on equal terms. That is a far more constructive approach than categorically saying no to something or presenting a one-sided view of the situation.

You could say to your boss: *When you give me a big assignment just before I'm about to head off in the evening, I feel obligated to stay late and get it done. I want to show that I'm a reliable team player and I sense that you expect me to turn it around quickly. But I have a real issue with this approach. I have obligations in the evenings that I need to attend to. I would like to discuss how we can come to a different arrangement going forward. How do you view the situation?*

As you find the courage to share your feelings and observations, you may come to learn the other person isn't deliberately trying to inconvenience you. You may also walk away with a solution that you hadn't anticipated prior to the conversation. Who knows? Perhaps the answer isn't that your boss stops handing you work late in the day but that you hire an assistant who can support you. For that reason, it can be helpful not to be too fixed on a specific solution in advance. The most transformational conversations happen when we suspend our judgements, listen, and ask open questions in addition to explaining our own side of the story.

Having these types of conversations is far from easy. Many of us haven't been taught how to express our needs, feelings, and expectations in an honest and balanced way and as a result we often hold ourselves back. We're worried it will upset or anger the other person, or that it somehow puts us in a bad light. But honest conversations don't have to be upsetting to anyone if we resist the urge to react, blame, justify, or deny. Those types of behaviors tend to divide rather than unite.

If you're worried about how the conversation will go, take time to prepare and practice how to articulate yourself. Thinking about what to say is good, but practice is even better. You can't predict how the other person is going to respond, but if you practice with someone you trust, they'll be able to give you feedback and help you adjust your message.

Truthful conversations are essential in looking after your own and other's emotional wellbeing. Opening up and sharing how you feel can be a great antidote to many stressful situations. It can actually be a great act of self-compassion and an effective way to take back your personal power. Issues build up in our minds and can quickly spiral out of control when based on assumptions and pent-up emotions. We need to bring them into the open, and address them in an emotionally balanced way before they consume us.

A friend of mine recently visited her elderly mother for her birthday and stayed in her home for a few days. On the day of her mother's birthday, my friend offered to cook her a beautiful meal and asked her mom to go and relax in the living room until the meal was ready. My friend, who had brought all the ingredients with her, started cooking the meal. The preparations were going well—the main dish was in the oven and the sides were perfectly timed so that they could be served together.

At this point the mother entered the kitchen. She saw the casserole in the oven and started complaining in a controlling and belittling tone because it was placed on the bottom rack. She opened the door to the hot oven in an attempt to rearrange the dish. My friend jumped to help her, worried that her mom would burn herself. She quickly grabbed a towel and pulled out the casserole dish from the oven. But because of the panic, and feeling the heat from the glowing dish, my friend accidentally dropped it on the floor. Not only was the birthday lunch ruined, there was also a hole in the newly laid kitchen floor.

When my friend and her mom finally sat down to eat, there was an awkward silence. My friend was angry at her mom for interrupting her cooking, for micromanaging her, and not trusting her to prepare the meal. Her mom was angry about the hole in the carpet.

The next day my friend decided to clear the air and have a calm and truthful conversation. This is what she said: "Mom, we have to talk about what happened yesterday. I had everything under control when you entered the kitchen and started micromanaging me. The way I had placed the casserole dish at the bottom of the oven wasn't wrong, but it's different to how you would normally do it. Where the dish is placed is not important. What happened to the floor is not important. I will pay for a repair. What's important is our relationship. I love you and I was cooking the meal as a gift for your birthday. I know this is your home, but there is no need for you to micromanage me. It's happened before and I would like you to stop doing that. It makes me feel angry that you can't trust me to cook a meal."

The beauty is that my friend found the courage to speak her truth and did it in a calm and considered manner while emphasizing how much she loves her mom. She resisted the temptation to lash out, and instead waited to talk about it until her own emotions were under control. By articulating how she feels when her mother micromanages her, she was able to express the impact on her, and to ask for her needs to be respected.

Dealing With Controlling or Aggressive Behavior

If a conversation goes as smoothly as you have planned, staying calm and clear-headed will be easy enough. It's much more difficult if the other person throws in a wildcard, starts to accuse you of something, or makes you feel small and intimidated. If you notice that their behavior triggers you, resist the urge to react from a place of anger or hurt because it won't serve either of you.

Keep your emotions in check as they may otherwise highjack you and get in the way of you getting what you really want.

You can manage your emotions by breathing as deeply and slowly as you can until you feel calm enough to get a perspective on the situation. Slow deep breathing, where you make the exhale longer than the inhale, is one of the most effective ways to slow down your heart rate and prevent your body and mind from going into a fight-or-flight response. It enables you stay connected with the most resourceful part of your brain, the prefrontal cortex. From that place you can consciously respond to what is being said rather than lashing out and letting yourself get provoked. We will explore in depth how to effectively make use of the breath in Chapter 4.

At the leadership programs I run, we often bring in actors who can help our participants practice how to have effective conversations with challenging clients and colleagues. By working with the training actors, our participants experience time after time how powerful silence can be. Just a few seconds of silence may feel like an eternity. But it works wonders when faced with aggressive or unacceptable behavior! Not only does silence send a strong message to the person you're communicating with, it's also an effective way to create a short gap in the conversation, thereby helping you manage your own emotions.

But silence is not the only answer. If your counterpart's behavior is unacceptable, for instance if they belittle you, or continuously interrupt you, you need to call it out and let them know how their behavior is affecting you. That's not always an easy thing to do—especially if you're speaking to someone in a position of authority. But it is a necessary step if you want to preserve your dignity, be respected, and be true to yourself. By way of example, you might say:

Kim, when you repeatedly interrupt me and speak over me, it makes me feel demotivated. Please can I ask that you let me finish my sentences. To have a constructive conversation, we need to listen to each other with an open mind and with respect.

Note that you're not actually blaming Kim for interrupting you, or saying that Kim is making you demotivated. Instead, you're pointing out what the effect of Kim's behavior is on you, and how it makes you feel. There is a difference.

If you struggle to express yourself clearly, notice how you feel in your body and what your unmet needs are. Perhaps you feel angry because the other person is speaking over you and is not respecting your views. Or perhaps you are overwhelmed by sadness and a feeling of not being good enough, because you have been accused of something that wasn't your fault. Whatever the unpleasant emotions, take note of them and feel them.

This kind of self-inquiry is a good starting point for considering what your part in the story is. In which ways might you consciously or unconsciously be contributing to what is happening? Controlling or bullying behavior cannot and should not be excused, but you need to understand if any of your own beliefs and behaviors contributed to it. Perhaps you are able to detect which beliefs and which part of your programming are at play here.

Many of us let ourselves be controlled by others, because we deep down feel that we aren't good enough. We don't believe in the strength of our own voice and end up handing our power to others. We may also have the feeling that conflict is bad, and therefore tend to avoid conflict or accommodate others because we are afraid to speak our truth. No wonder so many of us feel drained.

Expressing your feelings and observations to the person who you believe is controlling you, will be most effective if you understand what is going on with your emotions. Having this insight will help you stay true to yourself and articulate your views as clearly as possible without being hijacked by emotions. As you express your viewpoint, make sure that you don't exaggerate the issue or accuse the other person of mistreating you, even if you'd probably like to. Blame and accusations will only make your counterpart defensive and less likely to listen and empathize with you.

You're not trying to be aggressive and do to them what they did to you. Your goal is to be firm and strong and to help the other person understand how their behavior is affecting you. Imagine you are inviting them to walk in your shoes so they can see the situation from your point of view.

For instance, instead of telling the other person that their behavior is controlling or intimidating, which is an accusation, express what is happening at a practical and emotional level. You can do that by emphasizing what you are seeing, hearing, and feeling. You might say:

When you criticize me in front of our friends, it makes me feel angry, small, and unloved. I need to feel that you're on my side and that you have my back. Imagine how you would feel if I did the same thing to you. If you have the need to criticize me, can I please ask that you do it in private?

In this example the feedback is clear and firm, and not clouded by unnecessary emotion or blame. You simply express how their behavior is making you feel and that it's not acceptable to you.

Some people find it relatively easy to express their needs and set boundaries, whereas others find it very difficult, especially with people of authority. If expressing your authentic needs is a challenge, begin by practicing in situations where the stakes aren't so high, for instance when negotiating household chores or schedules in your home. In each situation, notice how you feel in your body and what your unmet needs are. Then practice expressing your truth in an emotionally balanced way. For instance:

Sweetheart, when I come home from work late and you talk to me at length about your day, I'm just too tired to listen properly.

That's frustrating for me because I want to be there for you. What I need is 15 minutes in silence to recharge my batteries. Is that okay?

When you're able to have these kinds of open and emotionally balanced conversations with friends, family, clients, and colleagues, you take back control and reclaim the energy that you had previously given up to the other person. You honor your authentic self and limit ongoing tension and energy drain. Firming up your boundaries and strengthening your regard for yourself are some of the most effective ways to safeguard your energy and your emotional wellbeing.[7]

Expressing Your Boundaries to Others Exercise

The goal of this exercise is to help you communicate your needs and boundaries to others. Doing so helps you reclaim your power, protect your energy reserves, and restore your self-worth. Set aside fifteen minutes for all three steps.

Step 1: Carefully consider the questions below in preparation for a conversation. Doing so will help you understand what you perceive the problem to be, what your real need is, and what you would like to achieve from the conversation.

- What is the specific topic or boundary you would like to discuss?
- What is your real need?
- How can you best explain your need?
- How would you like your relationship with the other person to be?
- What kind of mindset would you like to show up with?

Step 2: Now, turn the tables and reflect on how the other person might see the situation.

- What might the problem be in eyes of the other person?

- What are *their* underlying needs?
- What is *their* emotional state likely to be going into this conversation?

Step 3: If the person you'll be having the conversation with tends to be dismissive or aggressive, consider the following:

- Which part of their behavior could cause you to get activated or play small?
- How do you tend to react when you encounter this behavior? Do you blame and fight back? Do you withdraw and run away? Or do you give in and accommodate?
- How would you ideally like to respond to this person?
- What do you need to believe and say to yourself in order to choose this wise response?

CHAPTER 3:

Living by Your Core Values

"We are never more than a belief away from our greatest love, deepest healing, and most profound miracles."
— Gregg Braden

You might fall into the trap of feeling like you need to change your life entirely to feel more balanced and at ease, but that's not the case. There are almost always small adjustments you can make right away that will have a big impact. By substituting some of the things you do out of guilt, obligation, or boredom with activities that bring you joy and meaning, you can quickly change how you feel. That might mean starting to exercise instead of spending late nights in the office, going for a meditative walk or being in nature instead of watching something online, or spending more quality time with friends and family.

What makes the heart sing is different for everyone. While you might think you need to make a huge, expensive lifestyle change to feel different, often it's the small things in life that have the biggest impact on our wellbeing. That's because many of the small things bring us back to the present moment and away from our thoughts about the past or the future. Half an hour with your favorite book or playing your favorite instrument may be all you need to get above water. Once you feel more energized by your initial small steps, you'll have more space and energy to evaluate your life and take on larger changes if that's what feels right for you.

As much as we would all like to live a happy and meaning-ful life, it is unrealistic to expect to feel joy every single minute of every single day. No matter how hard you try, creating an environment of only energizing and fulfilling activities is not sustainable. Everyone experiences challenging moments, and curveballs can be thrown at us any moment. The more we accept that our journey will contain a mix of pleasant and unpleasant experiences, the easier it will be to handle difficult situations. Remember, accepting a negative experience is in itself a positive experience.

We all need some chaos, challenge, and discomfort in order to grow, and it's often our most challenging moments that con-tain the greatest opportunities for growth and transformation. Our default reaction may be to automatically turn away from a challenging situation, but, if we can instead open our heart and mind to the experience, there may be something in it for us to learn.

When we become curious and turn toward the difficulties in life, we will cycle through the unpleasantness with more ease and bounce back quicker. Later, we will explore this in more depth. We will look at how to increase our tolerance toward challenging circumstances and embrace unpleasant emotions. Ironically, it's when we're able to be in the unpleasantness, and step into the unknown, that true freedom can emerge.

Doing More of What You Truly Love

Right now, let's focus on getting to a place where a bigger pro-portion of your experiences are fulfilling and energizing. That means doing more of what you truly love so that you have more energy for yourself and others. Getting to that place requires you to deeply think about what it is in life that brings you joy and meaning. What is it that makes you laugh and what do you ab-solutely love doing? It also requires you to take this information seriously and start making small changes so that something will actually shift for you.

Maybe it's been a while since you spent time just on yourself. If you feel you're no longer in touch with your true desires, you can think back to a period of life when work wasn't as hectic and when home life wasn't as demanding. What used to bring you joy, energy, and meaning? It may help to close your eyes and use your imagination.

You may have noticed a little voice in your head reminding you of all the reasons why you're not currently doing the things that bring you joy and energy. The voice may say that you're working late and not getting to the gym because of your excessive workload. Or it may say that you're not getting time to see your friend or read your book because you're busy looking after your family. That may all be very true. But nothing will change unless you decide to challenge your level of thinking and make a change. No one can do it for you. You need to give yourself permission to make new choices, to reclaim your power, and to start building new habits.

Changing your level of thinking and making new choices requires conscious effort on your part. Remember, you first need to become conscious about your thought patterns, and then you need to be able to successfully override the patterns that no longer serve you. The vast majority of the time you're running unconscious programs that you downloaded from your parents and caregivers. Until you become sufficiently aware, you may be saying and doing things without really knowing why. You do them simply because that's the way you've always done them.

For example, if you would like to spend time attending art classes, but constantly find excuses for why you can't go, you'll have to question the level of thinking that's driving your behavior. Perhaps your existing belief is that you don't have enough time or money or that you're too tired to go. A new belief could be that your creative needs truly matter and that creativity helps you feel energized, joyful, and confident.

Creating a new habit and incorporating your new belief is easier said than done. But it is very possible when you put your mind to it and start small. Many of us make the mistake of setting unrealistic targets. We go for too many big changes at once, which invariably sets us up for disappointment because we set our expectations too high, too fast, too soon. We may decide to go to the gym every single day, but when we miss a day and don't live up to our own high expectations, we criticize ourselves and feel like we have failed. To avoid setting yourself up for disappointment, start with small, gradual changes and increase your stretch as you go along. Make it easy to celebrate your successes as you begin this journey.

Perhaps you start by setting aside fifteen minutes each day to go for a walk at lunchtime, or you get your crayons out and decide to spend a few minutes doodling at the end of the day. Applying the Japanese concept of kaizen (which is about continuous improvement), you add a few extra minutes of effort each day to your chosen activity, thereby gradually forming a strong habit. Wherever you decide to start, consistently do something each day that helps you feel good and come home to yourself.

Many of the people I coach have extremely demanding jobs and struggle to set time aside for activities that truly nurture them. My client Ellen is a busy manager and a mother of three young children. During our coaching sessions it quickly came up that she wasn't getting enough sleep. Nor was she finding time to sing and play her music, something "she needed to do every day in order to nurture her soul," as she put it. Ellen believed her kids weren't capable of making many of their own decisions, so she spent a lot of time planning detailed activities. All this extra work wasn't necessary and actually ended up disempowering her children. The same pattern played itself out at work. She believed she had to be on every single call and personally resolve every issue with the overseas subcontractors even if it meant staying up late to connect on their time zone.

Ellen's first step was to recognize that she needed a new strategy if she wanted to avoid burnout. Surviving on four hours of sleep and not having any time for herself wasn't sustainable. She knew she needed to protect her own energy today so she would have enough left over to be there for her team and family in the long run.

Changing her habits wasn't an overnight fix, but she gradually began turning things around. Her first action was to give more space to others and ask for help. She delegated some of her work calls, empowered her children to make age-appropriate decisions, and hired someone to make home-cooked meals. The big game changer however, was setting aside time each evening to sing and play her harmonium, even if the only convenient place to do so was in the garage. This one activity was the most rejuvenating and rewarding thing she could do for herself.

Another client of mine was in a very similar situation. As an HR manager she was doing the work of three people, and at home she was looking after her toddler. Her job was so demanding that she often had to be on calls after her toddler was put to bed. She was exhausted and told me that she felt broken. Her biggest issue was that she prioritized everybody else's needs over her own, and that she couldn't say no or ask for what she needed.

Like in Ellen's case, her first actions were two-fold. At work she requested that the late-night calls got moved to earlier in the day. And at home she practiced asking her husband for help in committing to her own self-care. All she needed was a set time a week when she could do sports while her husband would pick up their little boy from daycare.

Identify a Rejuvenating Activity Exercise

The purpose of this exercise is to become aware of the everyday activities that give you joy and meaning and to take a small first step toward a more energizing future. Beginning to incorporate more fun and rejuvenating activities into your daily life will improve how you feel about yourself and build momentum for larger changes that may lie ahead.

Set ten minutes aside for this activity right now.

Step 1: Settle into a comfortable place where you can feel totally relaxed. Then make a list of three activities you could potentially do on a daily or weekly basis that would make you feel happy and rejuvenated. Think of small activities that you love doing and that perhaps make you laugh or make you feel deeply connected to yourself.

Step 2: Pick one of the activities from your list and make a decision to incorporate it into your life. Perhaps it only requires 15 minutes of your time a day or an hour each week. Choose the activity that will have the biggest positive impact on your wellbeing and that requires the least amount of effort. Which first step will you take this week to incorporate it into your life?

Step 3: In order to carry through and continue to make more space for your chosen activity, consider which new beliefs you need to take on to make the change stick. Write down your old belief (e.g. *it's selfish to care for myself*), then strike it through and write your new belief next to it (e.g. *self-care is an essential part of my life*).

Identify Your Deepest Held Needs and Values

You can quickly reap the benefits of creating new meaningful habits. They will bring more joy and energy into your life. You will feel better and you will have more to give to people around you. You will also be in a better position to take a step back and evaluate your life in a broader sense. Having the courage and insight to change your life on a bigger scale can be near impossible if you feel drained and unhappy. It's much easier when you have momentum and feel energized by the small changes you have made.

To examine your life in a broader sense and investigate if larger and more fundamental changes are needed, it's necessary to uncover your core values. Values determine what's important to you and what you find meaningful. When you live by your core values, your life will be filled with purpose, which is what keeps you healthy and makes you jump out of bed in the morning.

The best way to inquire about your deepest held values is to reflect on the most important elements of your life. Simply bring to mind all the aspects that you value and all the elements that are important to you. This is about asking yourself what you must have in order to be fulfilled and identifying what you are truly grateful for. Examples of what you value could be children, fun, nature, friendships, food, travel, music, etc. There is no right or wrong. What makes the heart sing is different for each person. Some people love gardening. Others are into antiquities or science. Embrace what makes your heart sing, whatever it is.

You can also elicit your values by thinking about moments in your life when you felt particularly inspired and alive. When you bring to mind the happiest and most fulfilling experiences of your life and why they stand out to you, you will come to understand your core values.

When I bring to mind some of the most memorable experiences of my life, they often relate to times when I was travelling, experiencing new cultures, and exploring nature, all things I value dearly. I vividly remember river rafting in Turkey, trekking in Bali, canoeing past rhinos on the Zambezi, standing at the top of Machu Picchu, and experiencing a procession in a 3,000-year-old temple in India. In those moments I felt truly alive and high-spirited. That's because my needs for growth and feeling connected to the natural or spiritual world were fulfilled during those moments.

Interestingly, it isn't just the moments of joy and fulfillment that tell us what our core values are. Moments that fill us with dread and dislike also give us a clue because they signal that some of our most fundamental values weren't present. To live a truly fulfilling life, we have to allow sufficient space for our core values to be expressed. It's as simple as that.

In some of the workshops I run, I facilitate an exercise where the participants get to identify and prioritize the things that are important to them in their life. I first ask them to write down four of their biggest strengths, then four things that motivate them, four different people who are important to them, four achievements they are most proud, and four goals that are important for their future. In addition, they identify and write down one further element that's important and that hasn't yet been captured. In total they now have 21 important items written down.

What then follows is an elimination exercise, where they first have to remove the six least important items, then five further items, and lastly four, meaning that they end up with only the five most important elements across all the categories. Most participants report back that their achievements were amongst the first items to be eliminated and the names of people they wrote down almost always remained. It's an eye-opening exercise to most of our participants because they often prioritize work over family life, whereas in fact, it's the family that's the bedrock of their values.

After we have identified our core values, it can be very insightful to ask why each item is important. If gardening appeared on your list, what it is about gardening that makes it important? Is it about freedom, or does it make you feel more present and connected to yourself? In other words, what is the deeper level of fulfillment you get through gardening?

Likewise, if work appeared on your list, what is it about work that makes it essential? Is it related to recognition, challenge, security, or contribution perhaps? If your answer is that you work because of money, go one step deeper again by understanding what it is that money gives you. Keep peeling back the layers until you reach a list of words that reflect who you are at your core. Understanding why something is important to you helps you uncover the underlying needs you are seeking to fulfill and rediscover why you make the choices you make.

Many of us are driven by the need for safety, security, and certainty without being consciously aware of it. If we habitually opt for the safe choice, we may be motivated by an instinctual need for survival, even if we are not in any apparent danger. We may stay in a secure job or relationship and talk ourselves out of making exciting changes to our lives, even if those changes will help us grow and develop. Other people are completely opposite. They are driven by variety, change, and excitement. They like to do new things and enjoy taking risks.

Another basic need is the desire for love and connection, which shows up in values related to family, friends, and community. We all have this need, but we each seek to get it fulfilled in different ways. If we have a high need for love and connection, we would tend to feel most fulfilled in the company of others. Close relationships and feeling that we belong in a group are essential to every aspect of our lives. If we have a much lower relational need, we may feel satisfied living on our own and only occasionally connecting with close friends.

Another fundamental need is the need for significance. Deep down most of us want to feel important, unique, and special. We need to know that we matter and that our work and life are significant and distinctive in some way. We can fulfill this need in many ways, positive as well as negative. One way is by becoming a high achiever and having an important title or position, or by having possessions that make us stand out. A harmful way to attempt to meet this need would be to put other people down and elevate ourselves because we feel that we are (or need to be) better than others.

Other fundamental needs are freedom and autonomy. We all have a desire to make our own decisions, to pursue our own goals, and come up with our own ideas.

Growth and contribution are also fundamental needs. As human beings we want to learn and progress and contribute to something bigger than ourselves. These needs show up in values relating to learning new things, studying, self-development, knowledge sharing, giving back, and voluntary work.

All of these needs play a role in your life, but you will typically have two or three primary needs that are expressed through your core values and that influence most of your decisions. One of the needs that plays a big role in my own life is growth. I love learning, especially about health, spirituality, and personal development, and I value opportunities that help me learn and expand. I believe it's my need for personal growth that inspired me to train as a coach and leave my corporate career behind.

Many of the clients I work with come to coaching because they feel deeply unhappy and want to make a change. I've coached many people who didn't feel valued by their organizations and whose talents weren't being properly used or developed. In some cases, they worked for hard-hitting managers who, in spite of their cognitive intelligence, didn't know how to support and value their employees. In other cases, they worked in organizations that lacked vision, leadership, and integrity, giving employees little choice but to fight fires and work long hours to get the job done.

I've seen my clients make positive changes to their internal and external reality. In most cases, they found a new job that was better suited to their skillset and core values. But many employees also found happiness by staying with their existing employer. There will always be something about a job, relationship, or situation that isn't to our liking. To a certain degree, that's okay and perfectly normal. We can't always get what we want. The world doesn't exist simply to fulfill our individual needs. What's important is that our most fundamental needs and values are being met in some way. Otherwise, we won't be able to live our best and most fulfilling lives, nor will we be able to contribute to the best of our ability.

Not all of your needs have to be fulfilled by something or someone external to you. Imagine you have a high need for significance. You like to be seen and validated by people around you and are highly dependent on praise. Perhaps you didn't feel truly seen by your parents as a child and developed a strategy to get them to praise your behaviors. As an adult, you're still acting out this pattern and suffer emotionally when praise isn't given to you.

Rather than seeking to get this need fulfilled by other people, it would be far more liberating and satisfying if you learn to give yourself the recognition you so badly crave. Getting to that place requires you to go on an inner journey and learn to deeply love and accept yourself. That means loving the light in you as well as the darker aspects of your personality. That may well be the most rewarding journey you can make in a lifetime.

What Makes Your Heart Sing Exercise

The goal of this exercise is to create a list of all the things you truly value and to identify the reasons why they are important to you. When you become aware of your values and the underlying needs that drive these values, you will be able to evaluate the ways you have to adjust your life to feel truly fulfilled.

This is an important exercise, so set aside at least fifteen minutes for it. Make yourself comfortable in your safe and happy place, and make sure you won't be interrupted. Forget your to-do lists, give yourself permission to step away from your busy mind chatter, and let your creativity flow.

Step 1: Bring to mind all the aspects that you value in your life and all the elements that are important to you. What must you have to be fulfilled? What are you truly grateful for? Write down everything that has significance, for instance exercise, children, fun, nature, travel, music, etc. See if you can identify at least 10 items.

Step 2: Consider why each item on your list is important to you. For example, if travelling appeared on your list, what it is about travelling that makes it important to you? Is it about freedom, curiosity, variety, or is it about getting away from something heavy at home?

Keep asking why, and peel back the layers until you reach a list of words that reflect who you are at your core.

Step 3: Now, think about two or three of the most memorable experiences of your life—experiences that made you feel happy, fulfilled, and alive. Close your eyes and go right back in time. At what times did you feel an abundance of joy and meaning? Perhaps it was a family gathering, a holiday, a sports event, or a moment of achievement and recognition. Recall the imagery, the sounds, smells, and sensations associated with these happy and fulfilling experiences. What made them stand out to you? Can you see that each experience links back to the needs and values that are most essential to you?

Be the Change You Wish to See in the World

Purpose is a big word with a big promise. Studies show that people who live with more purpose benefit from better physical health and tend to live longer. Studies also show that those with a high sense of meaning are more engaged with families, colleagues, and neighbors, and they enjoy more satisfying relationships. They also tend to bounce back quicker from adversity because they are able to find meaning in the things that happen to them.[8]

The importance of having a purpose in life is also emphasized by Meghan Walker, a naturopathic doctor and CEO of Entrepology Labs. She says that out of her 2,976 patient files, those who identified as having a purpose in life had less recurrence of disease, they had less anxiety, and their energy levels were better over time. They also recovered with greater expediency than those who didn't have a clear purpose in life.[9] Can you think of any better reason to uncover who you truly are and bring your gifts into the open?

Purpose is not about your choice of career. It's about the meaningfulness of your life. Your purpose could be described as what you are ultimately here to do. It's your reason for living and it's completely unique to you. As an example, your purpose in life may be to help people in need, and there are multiple ways to support that purpose. You could for instance work as a doctor, a counsellor, or an aid worker, but being a doctor or an aid worker is not the purpose in itself. Your purpose is bigger than what you do for a living. It's what makes you jump out of bed in the morning and what keeps you healthy. Some people are here to teach and bring information into the world. Some are here to provide love, help, and healing, and others are here to shake things up and introduce new ideas and new ways of thinking.

When you live your purpose, it will feel like you're in the right place, doing the right thing for the right reasons. That can happen when the values you hold deep in your heart are expressed through your actions, in service to other people and the world. In other words, there will be alignment between what you think and feel on the inside and what you say and do on the outside. When you make use of your authentic gifts and dare to show the world who you really are, you will feel strong and grounded and filled with boundless energy.

Perhaps you are in a good place at the moment and feel that your inherent need for purpose is already being met, for instance through the family you're raising or through the work you do. Or maybe you feel something is missing and you would like to have a bigger impact and give back to your community or the planet. Perhaps you're becoming more conscious of how you live and how you affect people and the world around you. Perhaps you are also becoming more socially aware, more environmentally aware, and more aware of the power of your own heart and mind. That's a good thing.

"Be the change you wish to see in the world." Remember these wise words often attributed to Gandhi? It's a catchy phrase, which most likely originates from this particular paragraph of his: "We but mirror the world. All the tendencies present in the outer world are to be found in the world of our body. If we could change ourselves, the tendencies in the world would also change. As a man changes his own nature, so does the attitude of the world change toward him. This is the divine mystery supreme. A wonderful thing it is and the source of our happiness. We need not wait to see what others do."[10] Gandhi's words are well worth pondering on—*If we could change ourselves, the tendencies in the world would also change.*

Asking yourself which changes you wish to see in the world provides an excellent way to identify your higher purpose. What does an ideal world look like to you? What are your hopes for yourself, your family, society, and for the planet? Perhaps you imagine a world where all children have equal education and grow up in a safe home. A world where we have clean oceans, drinking water, soil, and air. Or a world where people show concern for their neighbor and take full responsibility for their actions. Let your mind be open to ideas, images, words, sensations, and notice what comes to you. Whatever resonates the most and whatever you feel most passionate about provides a clue toward your higher purpose. By embracing your purpose, you will challenge yourself to grow and evolve in meaningful ways.

Investigating who you are when you are at your best and what your innate strengths and skills are also provides a clue toward your purpose. For instance, who are you when you are doing something that comes effortlessly to you? And who are you when you forget time and space because you just love what you are doing?

It's important to mention that your purpose doesn't have to look a certain way or be grandiose or worldly. Raising a beautiful family, teaching in the local school, being fully present in your life, and being the best version of you are all examples of worthwhile purposes.

No matter how big or small your purpose, it will be something that helps you grow and evolve and that serves others. Jack Kornfield, a renowned meditation teacher and trained Buddhist monk, often talks about how we can serve by tending to the garden of the world. He says that you can't fix the whole garden, but you can pick your plot and where to plant your seeds.[11] It doesn't matter how big the garden is. At the end of the day, it's about how you feel and how you make others feel. If you wake up most mornings with feelings of joy and meaning, you're on the right path.

I recently met a young female monk who told me that her focus in life was to grow spiritually. She had no goals for how her life would develop in the physical world. She was committed to living a life of service in whichever way would serve her spiritual growth. If that meant she should teach, that's what she would do. If it meant she needed to travel or start a family, she would do that too. I found her openness to life and her alignment with her higher purpose to be very admirable and freeing.

Allow Yourself to Dream

It's possible that you won't be able to identify your purpose simply by using your rational mind. Perhaps you need to engage your intuitive mind and notice the feelings that arise when you see, hear, and feel the different imaginary scenarios. Paying attention to your feelings is the real guide to your intuitive intelligence. Allowing yourself to daydream is another important element.

When you allow yourself to dream, it can be helpful to think of yourself one or three years from now and imagine that everything has gone exactly the way you wished it would. By imagining yourself in a future place where all of your heart's desires have been met and you're contributing to the world in a deeply meaningful way, you can bypass the limitations of your conditioned mind. You simply imagine that everything will go exactly the way you hope it will, that all the right doors will open for you, and that your life will be filled with joy, love, and meaning. The idea is to open your heart and give yourself permission to feel how it feels to live in a place where you are totally at ease and where you are contributing to the world in a deeply meaningful way.

When you project yourself into the future it can be tempting to let your ego dream up a lavish lifestyle with lots of material possessions. But that's unlikely to fulfill you at a soul level. Empty dreams are generated by the ego, which tends to value things like money and prestige. The kind of vision you're after is one that rings true at a much deeper level. You want to connect to the authentic part of you and to imagine what your life would look like if you gave yourself permission to live according to your purpose and heartfelt values. Even if your conceptual mind doesn't have the answer, your heart and your inner wisdom knows what is right for you. You just have to be still enough to tune in to it.

As the vision of your desired future becomes clearer, you can set an intention that will bring you closer toward living your purpose. Your intention could be quite simple. For instance, spending more time in nature, being more present with the people you love, or providing a light in the darkness for those who are lost. Other examples could be to start a family, let your core values shine through in every interaction you have, or start a movement to create the kind of world you wish to live in. There is no right or wrong. You will know which action—be it big or small—can bring you closer to your heart's desire.

You may not be able to fully visualize your purpose yet, and that's okay. It can take time to discover your higher purpose, and it takes effort to steer your life in the direction that's right for you. As you go through life and gain new insight and experiences, your view of yourself and the world deepens. You mature, you let go of some of your baggage, and you may feel that you have more to offer to those around you. That's why it's so important to do the inner work and to heal your traumas from the past before you set out to change the world. As you mature, you are better able to open your heart and to give from the right place, not just to your inner circle, but to the world at large.

As it happens, we could be doing more harm than good if we jump into action, wanting to save the world, without having done the inner work. In his excellent book *Awareness*, Anthony De Mello writes, "many people swing into action only to make things worse. They're not coming from love, they're coming from negative feelings. They're coming from guilt, anger, hate; from a sense of injustice or whatever... You have to make sure of who you are before you act. Unfortunately, when sleeping people swing into action, they simply substitute one cruelty for another, one injustice for another."[12]

Don't hesitate to go deeply within yourself and discover your true essence. To live a fulfilling life and come back to your center, you have to go on an inner journey to honor and make peace with who you are. The journey will be worth it. Don't we all want to live a deeply meaningful life? If we ask those who are approaching death, it certainly seems so.

Bronnie Ware is a nurse who spent several years caring for patients at the end of their lives. In her highly acclaimed book *The Top Five Regrets of the Dying*, she has captured wisdom from those who were dying.[13] The biggest regret she heard from people was *I wish I'd had the courage to live a life true to myself, not the life others expected of me.* The other common regrets she recorded were: *I wish I hadn't worked so hard. I wish I'd had the courage to express my feelings. I wish I had stayed in touch with my friends.* And finally, *I wish I had let myself be happier.*

Don't allow yourself to have these regrets on your deathbed. You only have one life, and it's here to be lived.

Identify Your Higher Purpose Exercise

Set aside fifteen minutes right now for this exercise, which will help you connect to your inner wisdom. The idea is to allow yourself to have an ambitious dream on behalf of yourself and the planet and identify what your higher purpose might be. I will guide you through the steps. All you need to do is relax and open your heart and mind.

Step 1: Make yourself comfortable, and take a few slow, relaxing breaths. Breathe in through your nose and out through your mouth, letting go of any tension. Let your shoulders be loose, relax the small muscles in your face, and let your jaw drop. With each exhalation you let go of tension and become a little more relaxed. Sit for a few minutes noticing the subtle movements of your breath and the stillness of your body.

Step 2: Now, ask yourself the following questions and see what emerges:

- What does an ideal world look like to you?
- What do you really care about?
- What changes do you wish to see?
- What are your hopes for yourself, your family, society, and for the planet?
- Who are you when you are creative and making full use of your strengths and skills?
- Who are you when you forget time and space because you just love what you are doing?

Take your time exploring these questions and write down your findings.

Step 3: Imagine that two years from now you will be in a place where all your heart's desires have been met. Everything will go exactly the way you hoped it would. You feel strong and courageous, and you are contributing to the world in a deeply meaningful way. All the right doors have opened for you and you're honoring your innermost values. You are surrounded by people who you love and respect and you are of service to others, making a real difference. Your life is filled with joy and purpose.

Step 4. Open your heart and really imagine this future, where you are totally at ease and contributing to the world in a deeply meaningful way. Where do you imagine you will be one year from now? In which ways could you be of service to others?

The kind of vision you're after is one that rings true at a soul level, rather than dreaming up a lavish lifestyle with lots of material possessions. Trust that your heart and your inner wisdom knows what is right for you. You just have to be still enough to tune in to it. See if you can connect to the authentic part of you and imagine what your life would look like if you lived according to your purpose and heartfelt values.

Step 5. As the vision of your desired future becomes clearer, set an intention that will bring you closer toward living your purpose. Your intention could be quite simple. For instance, spending more time with your family, studying a topic you're passionate about, or contacting a local charity. There is no right or wrong way to begin. All you have to do is start with a small action that will bring you closer to your heart's desire.

The Power of Passion Circles

Your choice of career can play a major role in how you express your purpose and bring about the changes you wish to see in the world. What you do for a living can be a vehicle to pursue your vision. To better understand how you might express your purpose through your work, it can be useful to play with a technique I refer to as the passion circles.

Years ago, when I worked as a project manager in financial services, I was dreaming of making my passion more central to my work. At the time, my interest in personal and professional development was already sparked, and I had been using my coaching skills for several years in parallel with my day job. When I sat down and asked myself what I was good at, and what I loved doing, three passions emerged.

First there was my passion for my current profession. I enjoyed being a project manager and I was good at it. I also enjoyed working in a corporate setting. As much as I didn't feel fulfilled by it, I didn't want to turn my back on it completely. So, corporate project management was my first passion.

The second passion was coaching. My first experience with coaching at a leadership workshop inspired me so much that I decided to study and qualify as a coach. It was very clear that whatever I did with my life, coaching and professional development would have to be a part of it.

My third passion was wellbeing, which for me included physical, emotional, spiritual, and mental health. From a very young age I've been interested in eating nutritious foods and keeping my body in shape. Added to this came an interest in yoga and meditation, which I'd been increasingly captivated by over the years. As you can see, each of my three passions encompassed fairly broad categories.

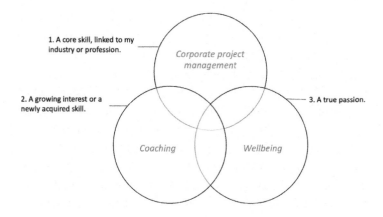

Looking at my passions, I then created three circles, one per passion, and began to investigate how they might overlap. I wanted all three passions to be part of my career, so what was the sweet spot between them all?

At the intersection between corporate project management and coaching, I found project management coaching, leadership coaching, and leadership development. That gave me a strong indication of the direction I needed to move in. I felt a strong desire to give up my full-time job as a project manager and instead begin to coach other managers and executives. I also wanted to facilitate leadership workshops, and with time, that's exactly what I did.

When I embarked on my new career as a project leadership coach, I was aware that I also wanted to incorporate my third circle—wellbeing. What do you get when you add wellbeing to the mix of project leadership coaching and leadership development? You might find coaching services that help managers overcome stress, or leadership programs that have an element of mindfulness to them. That was the space I was ultimately interested in and that I gradually began to expand into.

Like me, you can work toward integrating all three passion circles into the work you do. Rome wasn't built in a day, so don't worry if you can't get all three circles to fit right away. You can start with the first two and gradually ease yourself into the sweet spot where all three circles overlap. What's important is knowing the direction you want to go in, and why you want to go there, rather than having a detailed road map worked out. When your why is big enough, you will figure out the how.

I have used this technique with many of my clients, and it turns out to be a fun way of exploring how to integrate their passions into the work they do. I first ask them to draw three overlapping circles on a piece of paper, like a Venn diagram. Each circle refers to something they are good at and passionate about. The first circle represents a core skill they have and could be linked to the industry or profession they already operate in. It's the bedrock of what they do or would like to do professionally. Examples might be writing, engineering, teaching, designing, selling, event planning, communications, etc. It's important that it's something they're skilled at because this is the core service they are planning to offer.

The second circle represents another ability they have. It could be a growing interest or a newly acquired skill that they'd love to incorporate into their work. For example, sustainability, gardening, psychology, children's health, or online learning. Finally, the last circle would represent a true passion that they'd be delighted to make part of their work if possible. This could be topics that might seem a bit harder to integrate into your work. For instance, Spain, arts, cycling, food, etc.

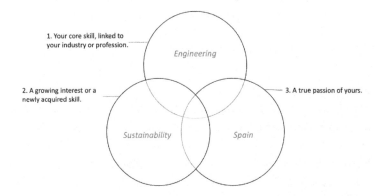

The power of the passion circles is to see what emerges when the three circles come together and overlap. Ideally, you'd like all three of your skills or passions to be a part of the work you do. For example, at the intersection of engineering, sustainability, and Spain, a wide range of options emerge, such as building sustainable houses in Spain. The combination of teaching, gardening and art could result in someone running workshops about the art of garden design or how to make use of sculptures in gardens.

Although the creation of the passion circles is a simple exercise, it can take a few attempts to identify what the right ones are, and what emerges when you combine them. As you brainstorm and evaluate the different possibilities, hold them up against your purpose and notice which of them would allow you to best express your purpose so you can be the change you wish to see in the world. Engage your intuitive mind and take each option into your heart and gut and notice if it resonates. It's an exciting process. Your inner guidance system will tell you when you're on the right path.

The Passion Circles Exercise

I invite you to get pen and paper out right now and start identifying your own three passion circles. The purpose is to be creative and to see what emerges in the space where your three circles come together and overlap. Finding the sweet spot between your three circles gives you invaluable information about how to express your purpose and bring about the changes you wish to see in the world. Set twenty minutes aside for this exercise and be prepared to come back and refine it later.

Step 1: Find a space where you can be creative and won't be interrupted. Then draw a Venn diagram with three overlapping circles.

Step 2: Looking at the first circle, identify your core skill, for instance linked to the industry or profession you already work in. This is the bedrock of what you do or would like to do professionally, and it's something you are already skilled at. For instance, fund-raising, marketing, acting, programming, teaching, etc. Brainstorm words that ring true for you and write them inside the first circle.

Step 3: For the second circle, identify another core skill you have or a growing interest that you would love to work with. This could be nature, holistic therapies, youth education, or anything else that you have a big interest in. Write this down inside the second circle.

Step 4: The last circle represents a true passion of yours. It's something that would make your heart sing if you could somehow incorporate this into your work. Allow yourself to dream and write down any words that come to mind inside the third circle. For instance, volunteering, surfing, handicraft, arts, traveling, etc.

Step 5: Now, look at the intersection between the three circles and identify creative options for incorporating all three aspects into your work. Play with it and see what themes come up for you. Engage your intuitive mind and feel into each option that emerges.

Which of the options would allow you to best express your values and live your purpose? Close your eyes and notice if any of the options create a warm tingling sensation in your body. Trust that your inner wisdom will tell you when you're on the right path.

Who Are You When You're at Your Best?

Let's take a moment to check in with how you are feeling right now. If you feel inspired to follow your passion and have already put the wheels in motion, that's great. It could also be that you feel confused and are filled with doubt and fear about the road ahead. Perhaps the limiting and anxious part of you is kicking in and disrupting your inspiring vision. Perhaps it's telling you that you can't have what you truly long for, that your dream is unrealistic, or that it's unsafe to make a change. What is the little voice in your head saying right now? And how do you relate to it? Do you argue with it? Do you try to shut it off or distract yourself so you don't notice it?

Keep in mind that this doubtful voice of yours is trying to protect you and keep you safe. There really is no need to turn your back on it. Instead, be curious, open up to it, and create a dialogue with it. You might even want to thank it for looking out for you. Then find out what this part of you is trying to protect you from. Which basic human need is the fear worried about and trying to safeguard? Is there an elegant way in which you can satisfy this need while continuing to move forward and pursue your passion?

Many of us would like to make changes in our lives, but we're playing small. We underestimate what we're capable of and we give in to the small fearful part of us. The negative voice grows bigger and the limiting thoughts begin to dominate. It's easy to get influenced by the stories we tell ourselves when our instinctive need for safety, security, and a sense of belonging kicks in. Our reptilian brain is designed to keep us safe so it is constantly scanning for threats. Whenever danger arises—be it real or perceived—we react with a fight, flight, freeze, or fawn response. Fear can easily get triggered and stop us from following through.

When I started out on my journey, I feared that I wouldn't be able to make enough money as an independent coach and leadership facilitator. My fear was trying to keep me safe, but in doing so it stifled me and hindered my progress. Using my rational mind I reasoned that, as long as I took the necessary action and did what had proven to work for others in a similar situation, there was no reason why I wouldn't be every bit as successful as those who'd walked the path before me. And even if I wasn't successful, it would still be a learning experience. If I failed miserably, at least I would have tried. That last belief really helped me. I told myself that there is no such thing as failure, only opportunities to grow and learn.

I also found inspiration in Marianne Williamson's frequently quoted passage. In *A Return to Love*, she writes;

"Our deepest fear is not that we are inadequate. Our deepest fear is that we are powerful beyond measure. It is our light, not our darkness that most frightens us. We ask ourselves, 'Who am I to be brilliant, gorgeous, talented, fabulous?' Actually, who are you not to be? You are a child of God. Your playing small does not serve the world. There is nothing enlightened about shrinking so that other people won't feel insecure around you. We are all meant to shine, as children do. We were born to make manifest the glory of God that is within us. It's not just in some of us; it's in everyone. And as we let our own light shine, we unconsciously give other people permission to do the same. As we are liberated from our own fear, our presence automatically liberates others." [14]

This passage made me think about why I was really holding myself back. It's true that I had a fear about the financial aspects of becoming self-employed, but beneath that, there was another limiting belief which Williamson so clearly speaks to.

To help you overcome your fears, it can be a great help to think of a time in your life when you took action in spite of discomfort and hesitation. It can be a time when you overcame your fear to speak up and did it anyway. A time when you ended a relationship, embarked on an adventure trip, or any other moment when you made a decision to move forward in spite of your reservations. By reminding yourself of that moment, and by noticing how your physiology and psychology changes, you will be able to identify your biology of courage.

Your biology of courage is how you feel when you rise above fear and when you are absolutely certain that you can achieve something. It incorporates how you stand, how you breathe, and how you feel when you step up to a challenge. Your ability to access this state at will can prove invaluable on your road to living your purpose. No one can do it for you. You are the only one who can mobilize the strength and willpower that exist within you. Luckily, there is an easy way to access this state and that is to repeat the very words to yourself that you have used in the past to overcome a challenge. Perhaps you said, *F**k it, just do it! If not now, then when?* or *I only live once.*

It's never too late to find your purpose, be true to yourself, and start doing what makes your heart sing. Tony Robbins says we tend to overestimate what we can achieve in a year and underestimate what we can achieve in a decade. Remember that you are already standing on a mountain full of strengths, skills, and experiences. You just can't see it very well because you're standing on it.

One of the other ways in which you can work with your fear and find calm is to connect to your need for meaning, growth, and contribution. We all have a need to learn, progress, fulfill our purpose, and contribute beyond ourselves. When you keep fueling these needs by envisioning the future you would like to create and feeling how fulfilling it would be, you will find the courage to step forward into the unknown. You will find a way to overcome your limiting beliefs and move forward on your journey in spite of fear.

In other words, when your why is big enough, the how will follow. So, keep focusing on the reason why you want to change and what would happen if you don't. Fast forward 20, 30, or 40 years. What will your life look like 20 years from now if you don't make the adjustments that you dream of? Which regrets would you have? In which ways would you not be growing and not be contributing?

Your Inner Resources

As you begin to move forward in spite of your fear, you can draw strength from resources that make you feel stronger, safer, and more connected to yourself. The more you become aware of the safe space that already exists within you, the easier it will be to face the uncertainty outside of you.

There are many kinds of resources, real or imagined, that can help you feel safe and strong. It could be a person who supports and protects you, an image you find soothing, certain words or phrases that inspire you, particular movements or postures that help you feel confident and grounded, or memories of places that have a calming effect on you. When you identify your inner resources, it's important that you don't just think about them intellectually. Really allow yourself to feel the feelings and sensations in your body.

You've probably noticed that I make a big deal out of getting you to feel where you experience emotions in your body and to allow yourself to feel them. That's because your mind and body are intricately connected. Emotions play a vital role in your overall wellbeing and they inform the actions you do or do not take. The better you are at noticing your emotions and how they present themselves in your body, the easier it will be for you to release unwanted feelings of fear and create feeling of safety at will. You cannot think your way to safety, courage, or self-love. You have to feel it.

Building on the somatic experience in your body, it can also be helpful to imagine being surrounded by a circle of allies and powerful protectors. The idea is to think of people who matter to you and whose support make you feel safe, strong, and confident. It could be close friends, business mentors, ancestors, superheroes, gods, or spiritual teachers. You can then imagine these beings joining hands and forming a protective circle around you. Doing so may enable you to feel their support, strength, and motivation radiating toward you.

I personally find it extraordinarily powerful to imagine my ancestors standing right behind me, so close that I can feel them physically holding me up and supporting my back. When I feel into this image, I get the sense that I come from a long lineage of torch bearers who are protecting me and supporting my back. No matter what happens, they will be there, right behind me.

Another beautiful practice is to put your feet flat on the ground and notice what that feels like. As you pay attention to your feet on the ground, you can begin to visualize long, strong roots growing from your feet deep into the ground connecting you with the earth. This connection with the earth will bring you strength, safety, and stability. With each in-breath these attributes of strength and courage flood your body from the ground below you. With each out-breath, your roots grow stronger and deeper into the ground, absorbing all of your tension. It's a truly beautiful and transformative practice.

If you struggle with visualization, you can use your sense of touch, smell, taste, or hearing to calm down an anxious nervous system. You can feel the weight of a gemstone in your hand, put a hand on your heart, smell the aroma of essential oils, or walk barefoot on grass or sand.

It's also possible to tap into feelings of safety, calm, and courage by listening to certain songs or sounds or by saying soothing phrases to yourself like: *I will always be there for you. I love you no matter what. I am strong and I am good enough. I feel safe and I know I will be fine.*

Last but not least, perhaps the most powerful method of them all is to deliberately deepen and slow down your breathing in a way that alters your physical, mental, and emotional state. With just a few rounds of slow breathing you can change your entire physiology from one that only sees danger to one that feels calm and safe. We will spend more time talking about how to effectively use your breath and how to handle challenging emotions, including fear and anxiety in Chapters 4, 5, and 6.

In later chapters we will also discuss how to create a healthier relationship with your negative self-talk and how to challenge the many thoughts that swirl around in your mind. The question you need to answer right now however is; what kind of resources can you draw upon to make you feel safe, strong, and confident moving forward and living your purpose?

By tapping into your inner resources of strength and safety, you'll find it easier to commit to taking one small step in the direction of your vision every day. You don't need to have it all figured out or have a perfect plan of how your life will look in five years. All you need is to get the direction right and to take one small step each day. Imagine that right now. See yourself taking the first step toward your new future of serving the world and your soul's purpose. Small incremental steps are the most sustainable way to make a lasting change.

Identify Your Inner Resources Exercise

The purpose of this exercise is to identify your most powerful resources that make you feel safe and supported so you can maintain and build your strength for the journey ahead. Whenever you feel emotionally off center, or you need strength and courage to move forward, you can make use of these resources. Set five minutes aside to identify them right now.

Step 1: Think about someone or something that makes you feel safe, strong, valued, or courageous. It could be an object, a person, an animal, a gesture, a song, a smell, a phrase, a landscape, or a memory.

Step 2: As you bring to mind your resource, see if you can link it with as many sensations as possible. Which imagery, feelings, sounds, smells, or tastes do you associate with this resource? Don't just think about it. Feel it. Also notice how your emotional and physical state change when you bring to mind your resource. Are you able to feel strength, love, or perhaps courage rising from within?

Step 3: Now, identify the names of five persons or beings who make you feel strong, safe, supported, and courageous. It could be close friends, business mentors, ancestors, superheroes, gods, or spiritual teachers. Write down their names, then visualize them in your mind's eye. Imagine them joining hands and forming a protective circle around you. Notice how close they are to you—right in front of you and behind you. Feel their support, strength and motivation radiating toward you.

How do you feel right now? Are you ready to move forward with the support of your allies and inner resources?

CHAPTER 4:

Using Your Breath to Come Home to Yourself

"Breathwork is a way to rewire the nervous system and to tune in to our hearts. It's a way to come home to ourselves and to redefine who we are and what is possible."
—Stig Severinsen[15]

Well done for having come this far! Up until now we have explored how to create a life that matches your strengths, values, and desires. You have discovered how to show support and compassion for yourself, say no to the things that drain you, and infuse more joy and energy into everyday life. You have also become aware of the beliefs that limit you and discovered how to contribute to the world in deeply meaningful ways.

Now, it's time to explore how breathwork can help you find peace in the inevitable discomfort and messiness of life. As you progress on your journey of growth and self-discovery, you will encounter events, thoughts, and emotions that trigger you and throw you off course. These challenges don't necessarily mean you are journeying in the wrong direction or that there is something wrong with your life. It could simply be that you need to sit with, and deeply breathe in to, what is happening. The breath can help you relax into whatever is going on for you. When you're able to do that, you can access the beauty and stillness that exist regardless of day-to-day problems, stresses, and anxieties.

Initially, when you try to slow down and connect more fully with yourself and your breath, you may not feel calm and peaceful at all. Instead, you may be confronted with upsetting thoughts and emotions that you've been ignoring or avoiding. These thoughts and emotions could stem from painful memories you haven't yet processed, unresolved anxieties about the future, or existential concerns about mortality and the meaning of life. Sometimes we feel awfully vulnerable and uncomfortable when we sit still and don't do anything.

Being confronted with a layer of upsetting thoughts and emotions shouldn't be a deterrent to spending time in stillness and observing the breath. On the contrary, the breath plays a key role in helping us process whatever comes up. It can seem counterintuitive, but when we turn toward something that is upsetting and breathe deeply into it, the upsetting emotions will loosen their grip on us. The challenge is to keep breathing consciously and to get closer to ourselves, no matter what comes up. In that way we will eventually be able to dissolve the blockages and come into balance. When disturbing thoughts, memories, and emotions subside, the possibility to reach deeper states of relaxation opens up. Through breathwork, we can even reach deeper states of consciousness.

How good are you at being still and letting go of doing activities? Can you enjoy simply being with your breath, listening to it and embracing the present moment, even if strong emotions come up?

Many of us cling to our busyness and are addicted to living a busy lifestyle. Have you ever wondered why that is? How come we so often prioritize work and doing-activities over rejuvenating being-activities? Is it because we are driven by the need to achieve great things, to be seen, to be accepted, and to show the world that we matter? Or is it because we're afraid of what will happen if we stop for a moment?

Years ago, when I was first introduced to the idea of paying attention to my breath, I really struggled with my thoughts and feelings. I could only follow the flow for a few breaths before feeling impatient and beginning to engage with one of the many thoughts in my mind. At the time I was mostly living from my neck upwards and found it near impossible to get in touch with my body. I didn't realize how much I was missing out on by staying in my head. Most of us are taught to live this way. We learn to cut ourselves off from our body to avoid intense feelings. Distracting ourselves with thinking and doing activities is a survival mechanism that helps us cope with the things we find painful. But this way of coping can keep us disconnected from our true selves and stuck in old patterns.

If you've spent decades not being fully connected with your body and emotions, you have to understand that it will take a little practice to get back in touch and learn a different way of living. Instead of giving up when it gets hard, you need to give yourself the gift of patience and self-compassion.

Being present with my breath became easier over time as I learned to focus inwards, notice the sensations in my body, and allow whatever was happening emotionally to happen without trying to change it or stop it. I had to learn to open up to my feelings and pain. The practice of yoga also helped me on that journey. It taught me to slow down, be present with myself, and notice subtle movements and sensations in my body. In that sense, yoga was instrumental in assisting me to get out of my head and connect more fully with other parts of myself, physically, emotionally, and spiritually.

Today, I'm able to feel a deep sense of calm when I sit and just breathe, but it doesn't always happen immediately. First, I need to quiet my mind and distance myself from the many thoughts that race around. To get out of my head, I find it helpful to shift my focus toward my body. I may for instance relax my shoulders, notice my feet on the ground, or feel the weight of my body on the chair. I may also become aware of my heartbeat and listen to the sound of my breath as I inhale and exhale. It's a simple and powerful method that helps me become present with myself and break out of repetitive thought-patterns.

I sometimes find it helpful to imagine hearing the waves of the ocean. I find this very soothing, probably because I grew up by the sea and feel deeply connected with it. As a teenager I spent hours walking along the beach with my dog, confiding in the sea, and I always felt calmer at the end of my walk. When I practice the ocean breath, I slightly constrict my throat muscles, which creates a sound like waves on the ocean (or like Darth Vader). I normally close my eyes and imagine the waves coming and going on the shore. I hear them, I see them, and I become them.

As you spend quiet time with yourself and connect more fully with your body, a few things may happen. You could become really relaxed and calm right away because your attention is shifting and you're paying less attention to your thoughts. If that happens, then that's great. Just enjoy it. You've successfully taken a little break from your thinking mind and found relaxation and peace within.

As you shift your attention away from your thoughts, you might get confronted with a layer of built-up emotions that want to be heard, processed, and released. That could be anger, sadness, grief, fear, or any other emotion. If this is your experience, that's perfectly fine too. Don't resist it. Emotions come up because they need to be expressed and acknowledged. Sit with whatever comes up and continue to breathe deeply and rhythmically.

I sometimes have a wave of emotions come up, especially if I have been very busy for a while and haven't taken the time to check in with myself. I may feel sad without any apparent reason, or I may notice a strong sense of restlessness. When that happens, I do my best to acknowledge the emotion and simply let it be there. I try not to intellectualize it or rationalize it. Intellectualizing our emotions is when we spend all our attention thinking about our feelings (or thinking about the situation that led to our feelings) instead of actually feeling them. It can be a defense mechanism that helps us feel safe, but ends up keeping us stuck with unprocessed emotions.

Instead of intellectualizing, I bring my attention back to my feet on the ground and to my breathing. I also tell myself that my emotions aren't wrong and that the experience I'm having is the one I'm meant to have. That makes it easier to allow whatever comes up to be there without trying to fix anything. Eventually, the emotions pass, like clouds in the sky.

Embrace the Challenge of Sitting Still Exercise

I invite you to try a five-minute experiment with me right now. It's an experiment that will help you connect with your body, be more present, and practice sitting still.

- Sit up straight and place your hands on the side of your body just below your ribs.
- Take a deep breath in and let it go.
- Begin to inhale and exhale slowly through your nose.
- Notice how your abdomen and lower ribs expand into your hands as you breathe in, and how your spine lengthens and straightens as you breathe out.
- Continue breathing in a slow and rhythmic way for at least five breaths.
- Focus on how your core expands as you slowly breathe in and how your spine lengthens as you gently breathe out. Take your time.
- Now bring your attention to the base of your spine.
- In your mind's eye, slowly move your attention up the spine, vertebrae by vertebrae, until you reach the top where it attaches to the skull.
- Then reverse the flow. Slowly follow your spine from the very top, toward the base.
- Fully connect with your spine and notice how it moves as you breathe in and out.

What do you notice as you breathe this way? Does your body feel lighter and more relaxed? Or does something else happen? If emotions come up as you do this exercise, just accept them and feel them. You don't have to change anything. Remember, the experience you're having is the experience you're meant to have.

If you find it hard to sit still and focus inwards, don't worry too much about it. Most likely, gentle movement or a quiet walk will help you tune in to yourself and your breath.

Becoming More Conscious of Your Breath

Breathwork is one of the most powerful, quick, and accessible ways to help you center yourself whenever you feel tense, emotional, or stressed. If you learn to breathe with awareness, it can change how you think and feel in an instant. You may have already noticed how calming it can be when you take a deep breath in, followed by a long, slow exhale. That's because the mind and the body are intimately connected, and your breath plays a key role in regulating your nervous system. Your breathing influences your physiology, your biochemistry, your cognitive function, and your emotions, and vice versa.[16] That's very empowering because it gives you back some control of how you feel physically, emotionally, and mentally. Your breath is like a lever that you can pull at any time to change your nervous system and function better, whether you feel overwhelmed with stress or just trying to think of a solution to a work problem.

In a practical sense, the breath can help you let go of limiting thoughts, prepare for a challenge, calm down your nervous system, awaken your intuition, and increase your awareness of yourself and others. The renowned pioneer in breathwork, Dan Brulé writes in his book, *Just Breathe*, "The more conscious we become of our breath, the more conscious we become of everything: our thoughts and feelings, our habits and patterns, our posture, our behavior, other people's energy, our surroundings, and so on."[17] Not only can breathwork change your emotional state in a matter of seconds, it can also be a great tool for self-discovery.

Becoming more conscious of yourself and your surroundings is an essential step in coming home to yourself. When you become conscious of a limiting thought, for instance, you can explore it, question it, and choose a more supportive thought. On the contrary, when you're not conscious, you're operating on autopilot, unaware of the programs and beliefs that steer your every move. When that's the case, you're more likely to get trapped by unhelpful ways of thinking and behaving without the ability to be flexible and creative.

A good practice that can help you become more conscious is to set aside five to ten minutes each day for actively watching your breath without changing it. Simply sit and let the breath breathe you without interfering. Notice the sensations in your body and how you relate to your breath. You may for instance notice that your breath is either deep or shallow, fast or slow, rhythmical or choppy. The way you breathe in any given moment can tell you a lot about your emotional state and how you relate to life.

You can also watch your breath during the day as you go about your usual activities and interact with others. Notice how you breathe when you are relaxed and peaceful, when you are upset, angry, or afraid, and when you are nervous, tense, and stressed. What you will find is that your breathing changes dramatically over the course of the day, and even sometimes from minute to minute. With that awareness you can learn a lot about yourself and you can begin to actively make changes to your breathing to calm and center yourself.

In my own life I do my best to consciously pay attention to my breath. I become particularly aware of it when I feel stressed or tense and want to change my emotional state. In those moments, I relax my shoulders and my abdomen, and I focus on slowing down my breathing. I also try to make my outbreath longer than my inbreath. This instantly shifts my focus away from stressful external events to embracing the present moment. It could be any situation, big or small: waiting for a taxi and worrying I won't reach the airport in time, running late for a meeting, getting ready for a keynote speech, receiving news that's upsetting, or a client cancelling on me at the last minute.

You don't have to wait for challenging events to experience the transformative effects of breathwork. You can proactively bring to mind some of the limiting thoughts, memories, and insecurities you identified during the first part of this book, and consciously breathe into them. Instead of ruminating about these thoughts, or holding your breath when you think of them, you can loosen up and relax into them. You literally slow down your breathing pattern, and adjust your posture, thereby signaling to your brain and body that you are safe and there is nothing in your environment to be stressed about or afraid of.

Breathing Through Your Limitations Exercise

This five-minute exercise is most powerful when you experience a challenge that causes you to feel emotionally upset or off center. The purpose is to regulate your physiology by consciously changing how you breathe. When that happens, you will feel calmer because you're signaling to your body that you are safe.

Step 1: Bring to mind a thought, event, or image that causes you to feel stress, fear, or tension in your body. If nothing comes to mind, think of a change you would like to make that fills you with doubt or fear. For instance, what is your biggest fear in living the life you dream of? What is holding you back?

Step 2: As you bring to mind this unpleasant thought, image, or limitation, notice how your body contracts and your breathing becomes more rapid or rigid. Perhaps you even stop breathing when you feel into the unpleasantness.

Step 3: Continue to focus on the event that causes you discomfort and begin to deliberately slow down your breath. Relax your shoulders, soften your abdomen, and listen to the sound of your deep and slow exhale.

Step 4: Breathe as slowly and deeply as you can for a few minutes and notice the effect it has on your mind and body.

When you breathe this way for a couple of minutes, you begin to actively change your physical and emotional response to this limitation. You're effectively teaching your body that everything is well and that it's possible to relax, even if your body instinctively wants to contract.

How the Breath Affects Your Nervous System

Dr. Gerbarg, a Harvard-trained psychiatrist, explains that we can use the breath as a direct portal of entry into the autonomic nervous system, and from there into the brain control center. When we change the pattern and pace of our breathing, she says, we change the messages that the body sends to the brain. So even if we can't convince ourselves intellectually of something, our body can convince our brain for us. If you experience a panic attack for instance, simply saying to yourself, *I shouldn't be afraid*, probably won't work. But if you slow down your breathing and emphasize a long exhale, your body will signal to the brain that it's safe, and everything will calm down.[18] Breathing this way is one of the most powerful antidotes for anxiety and overwhelming thoughts and feelings.

Modifying your breath, even for a few minutes, can have a profound effect if you feel stressed, anxious, or afraid. When your brain detects danger, whether real or imagined, your sympathetic nervous system triggers the body's fight-or-flight response. This part of your nervous system is constantly on the look-out for threats and is programmed to help you get ready for action. You can think of the sympathetic nervous system as the gas pedal that speeds up your system. When it detects a threat, its default is to release stress hormones into the blood stream. When that happens, your breathing becomes rapid and shallow, your heart beats faster, your pupils get larger, your liver releases glucose, and your muscles tense up, ready to help you fight or flee.

Your body's stress response is instinctual and powerful. During a true emergency it can save your life in a split second. The issue isn't your body's fight-or-flight response, or how it reacts to short-term stress. You absolutely need this built-in safety mechanism for true emergencies. The issue is that your sympathetic nervous system may get triggered unnecessarily and too often. Not only can that have severe consequences for your physical health, it's also in direct opposition to feeling peaceful and coming home to yourself. When you're angry, upset, or anxious, you'll be feeling anything but centered, calm, and peaceful.

Another undesirable consequence of continually triggering your body's stress response is that your ability to think clearly and make rational and creative decisions is much worse. When the sympathetic nervous system is activated, it drains away resources from the prefrontal cortex, the seat of your rational and executive decision making. As your body prepares itself to fight, your focus will narrow, you will become more reactive, and your ability to think expansively decreases. No matter how high your IQ is, you won't be at your best intellectually or creatively when stress hormones are being released and your body is in fight-or-flight mode.

During an average day, you may be exposed to all kinds of stressful thoughts and events that trigger this kind of automatic fight, flight, freeze, or fawn response in you. You may have financial worries, health concerns, or conflicts with colleagues and family members. You may lock yourself out of the house, worry about the state of the world, or get anxious when faced with too much change or uncertainty. Or you may feel tense because of the many commitments and obligations you have. These aren't threats that will endanger your life, but your nervous system can interpret them as threatening.

In addition to the short-term impacts, there are serious long-term implications of operating in a heightened state of stress. After months of being in high alert, your elevated levels of stress hormones begin to play havoc with your body and mind. You can think of it as a form of adrenaline poisoning. You may begin to feel moody and exhausted. You may have difficulty sleeping or you may find it hard to focus. You may also have aches and pains and begin to notice that your body is finding it hard to repair itself. What's happening is that your body is so focused on fighting the perceived threats in your environment, that it doesn't have much energy left for internal maintenance. That's how you end up with a compromised immune system. The more resources your body needs to spend mobilizing external defenses, the less it can allocate to the internal immune response.[19]

Chronic stress is a serious issue that needs appropriate attention. Dr. Bruce Lipton, stem cell biologist and author of *The Biology of Belief,* states that up to 90% of all illnesses could be stress-related.[20] His breakthrough studies on the cell membrane of the human body revealed that genes can be switched on and off depending on the environment of the cell. In other words, in the majority of cases, it's not our genes that cause disease but our response to the environment. If we are putting undue stress on our system because we are out of alignment, have run out of energy, eat the wrong foods, and are busy fighting external threats, we are not providing our cells with the optimal environment they need to thrive and repair themselves.

Unfortunately, many of us aren't conscious of how much tension we carry, and we don't take our stress levels seriously.

We may not even feel stressed because we've become used to operating in a state of high alert. I know that this has been true for myself. During busy periods of my life, I can be in a go-go-go mode from the moment I wake up. I have so much drive and so much I want to do. The adrenaline gives me a boost of energy and it keeps me going. But if I stay in this mode for too long, it becomes harmful. I need to deliberately use my breath to come back into balance and plan for sufficient breaks so that my body, mind, and spirit can rest and recover.

Stimulating the Parasympathetic Nervous System

To calm down your nervous system, you have to stimulate the *parasympathetic* system, which is responsible for your body's rest, digest, and recovery processes.[21] If you think of the sympathetic nervous system as the gas that speeds up your bodily functions, then the parasympathetic nervous system[22] is the brake that slows you down. After a period of high alert, the parasympathetic carries signals that return your systems to their standard activity levels. In other words, it keeps the organs and basic functions of your body working as they should, but it's only able to do so when you feel calm and safe.

One of the most effective ways to stimulate the parasympathetic nervous system is to take slow deep breaths and to extend your exhale so that it's longer than your inhale. Taking full, deep breaths that expand your lower ribs and belly calms your nerves and reduces anxiety. And when your exhales are longer than your inhales, you slow down your heart rate automatically. In fact, every time you inhale your heart speeds up, and as you exhale, it slows down. This kind of deep, slow breathing has been shown to stimulate the vagus nerve, which is the largest nerve of the parasympathetic nervous system.

The more time you spend stimulating the vagus nerve and the parasympathetic nervous system, the quicker your mind and body will bounce back from stressful situations and build resilience. As your physiology changes and your blood flow shifts, you'll be able to think more creatively, digest your food better, and repair your muscles. This is a radical act of self-care.

One particular practice that has gained attention is the 4-7-8 breath.[23] Here, you breathe in to the count of 4, hold your breath to the count of 7 and breathe out to the count of 8. No matter how fast you count, it's important that your out-breath is twice as long as the in-breath.

Not only does this kind of breathing help you feel calmer and more centered, it also disrupts your pattern of negative inner dialogue. When you focus on your breath and on the counting, you get out of your ruminating mind and into your body, even if just for a few minutes. As Dan Brulé says, "It's almost like a mind trick: when you are focused on your breathing, when you are breathing consciously, then you're not focused on what would normally limit or control your thinking. When you focus on your breath instead, something new, something else is possible."[24]

Another interesting technique that you can benefit from in a matter of seconds, is what Andrew Huberman refers to as a physiological sigh. Scientists have found that two rapid inhales through the nose (the first slightly deeper and longer than the second), followed by one long, extended exhale through the mouth, allows for the most rapid reduction in stress levels. It's a breathing pattern which offloads the maximum amount of carbon dioxide and which children do spontaneously when they sob.[25]

The Huberman Lab found that just one, two, or three of these physiological sighs are enough to quickly bring our levels of stress down. They also studied people who used this breathing pattern for only 5 minutes a day and found that they had the greatest improvement in mood, lowered resting heart rate, and sleep compared to the control groups. I can certainly testify to the effectiveness of this technique. I feel something shift immediately when I take just a few of these types of breaths.

Breathing to Decrease Your Stress Exercise

Set five minutes aside to decrease your stress levels by practicing the 4-7-8 breath. Using this technique can help you feel calmer and more centered, and it also disrupts your pattern of negative inner dialogue. When you lengthen your exhales, you stimulate the vagus nerve and shift your nervous system toward parasympathetic dominance. And when you focus on your breath and on the counting, you get out of your ruminating mind and into your body.

- Take a deep breath in through your nose to the count of four.
- Hold your breath to the count of seven.
- Slowly let out the air through your mouth to the count of eight. If it feels right, add a long releasing sound to your exhale –AAAAAAAAH, or WUUUUUUU.
- Repeat the 4-7-8 breath for a few minutes. Breathe in to the count of four. Hold to the count of seven. Exhale to the count of eight. With each exhale feel how you soften and let go of whatever has been causing you tension.
- If distractions or worries come into your mind, allow them to come. Then allow them to go and bring your attention back to your counting and your breathing.
- After a while you may notice that your thoughts become distant and that you feel calmer and more balanced. That's because you're signaling to your nervous system that it's safe to calm down and relax.

How did you find this exercise? Were you able to detect a change in your physiology and in your state of mind?

Coherent Breathing

Reaping the benefits of proper breathing doesn't have to take much time. One study found that just two minutes of slow breathing at six breaths per minute led to a decrease in blood pressure among people with hypertension.[26] Another study of healthy adults found that five-minute periods of deep breathing at seven breaths per minute led to significant improvements in pain detection and tolerance.[27] Many other studies have shown that with anything from 30 seconds to 15 minutes of deep, slow breathing you can thoroughly recharge your batteries, improve your sleep, and lower your levels of anxiety, depression, and stress.[28]

To access these benefits, you will have to lower the number of breaths you take to only five or six slow breaths per minute. That's in stark contrast to the twelve to eighteen breaths per minute the average person takes. It appears that taking too many breaths can lead to depletion of essential minerals, which in turn can cause issues with the nerves, muscles, and bones.[29] How many breaths per minute do you tend to take when you breathe normally?

Several studies show that the optimal breathing pattern for most of us is 5.5 breaths per minute. That's 5.5 second inhales and 5.5 second exhales.[30] This breath—often referred to as Coherent Breathing—will make you feel calm, yet energized and responsive. It's not a breath you want to use if you have difficulties going to sleep. You want to use it for day-to-day interactions, problem-solving, and decision-making.

In addition, some people find it helpful to put a hand on their heart, close their eyes, and repeat soothing phrases to themselves as they practice breathwork. For instance, *I breathe in clarity and strength. I breathe out stress and tension. I breathe in courage and energy. I breathe out worry and confusion.*

To reap the full benefits of Coherent Breathing, breathe in slowly through the nose while allowing the abdomen and lower ribcage to rise. And as you breathe out, let your ribcage and abdomen flatten without any effort. This is how you get the most oxygen into the bottom part of your lungs. You want to avoid expanding your upper chest and moving your shoulders too much. If your breathing is fast and only your upper chest is moving, it may be a sign that your body and mind are in high alert. This way of breathing can lower the immune response and create tension in your neck and shoulders.

If you spend most of your day sitting down, try not to slouch as it makes healthy breathing more difficult. Poor posture can impact your ability to think clearly as the brain requires more oxygen to function optimally than any other organ or muscle.[31] When you sit at your desk, you want your spine and shoulders to be in an upright neutral position to make it easier for your abdomen to expand as you breathe.

Remember to always inhale through the nose. It's been proven that it stimulates parts of the brain that are responsible for memory and emotional processing in ways that mouth breathing doesn't.[32] If you want to dive deeper on this topic, look no further than James's Nestor's best-selling book, *Breath*, where he measured the harmful effects on his own body by exclusively breathing through his mouth. He completely plugged his nose with silicone for 10 days, confessing that it wasn't a pleasant experience. "I developed sleep apnea" he says. "My stress levels were off the charts. My nervous system was a mess. ... I felt awful. I still have a little PTSD about it all."[33]

Coherent Breathing Exercise

Set five minutes aside right now to practice Coherent Breathing. The benefit of this breathwork technique is to balance your nervous system so that you can experience being alert and calm at the same time.

- Take a slow and soft breath in through your nose while counting to five or six without straining yourself.
- Slowly and softly let go of your breath to the count of five or six.
- To help keep the rhythm, it may be helpful to imagine that, as you are breathing in, you draw a half circle around your body and, as you breathe out, you complete the other half of the circle. You can also find apps or videos on the internet that help you keep the rhythm.[34]
- Continue to breathe continuously for a few minutes without pausing between in-breath and out-breath.
- Make your breathing deep, soft, and rhythmical, actively drawing in the breath and passively letting it out. The goal is to make it a ten or twelve-second rhythm, so that you take between five and six breaths per minute.
- To check that you're breathing correctly, place one hand on your upper chest, and the other on your abdomen just below the rib cage. You want to avoid expanding your upper chest and moving your shoulders too much.
- If you have difficulty detecting which parts of your chest and abdomen are moving, you may find it easier to practice lying down.

Alternate Nostril Breathing

Another breathwork practice that can help you come into balance is alternate nostril breathing, a technique commonly taught through yoga. It's a practice where you alternate between breathing in through the right and left nostrils. It's an effective way to naturally slow down your breath and create deeper states of relaxation. When my mind is racing, I find this practice particularly useful. It gives my monkey mind something specific to do because I have to pay attention to doing it right.

In Ayurvedic medicine and yoga, it's thought that alternate nostril breathing helps stimulate and balance the activity of both hemispheres of the brain, resulting in physical, mental, and emotional wellbeing.[35] [36] It turns out that when you breathe in through the left nostril and out through the right, you stimulate the parasympathetic rest, digest, and recover system. Similarly, when you breathe in through the right nostril and out through the left, you stimulate the sympathetic nervous system, which puts the body in a more elevated state of alertness and readiness.[37] [38]

If you are new to breathwork or alternate nostril breathing it might take you a little while to get used to this technique. If you find that it brings you benefits, you can experiment with it and challenge yourself, for instance by breathing to the count of 4-4-8. Inhale through the left nostril on four, hold your breath on four, and exhale through the right nostril on eight. Then you repeat with the right nostril. If you find this easy, you can take it even further by holding your breath for longer. The slower you breathe and the longer you are able to hold your breath, without getting dizzy, the greater benefits you may experience.

Stig Severinsen, the founder of Breatheology and a world freediving champion, says that, if you learn to hold your breath for longer, you will gain more energy, become calmer, and more resilient to stress. Part of the explanation is that when you resist the urge to breathe, you are effectively practicing how to stay calm under pressure. You are deliberately exposing your body to a stressful event and learning how to consciously relax at the same time. With practice, you can train yourself to stay calm and focused when faced with stressful situations during the day.

In a similar vein, breath-holding can help you work through deeply rooted emotional issues that you may have to confront. That's how Stig is able to help veterans overcome severe episodes of PTSD. When you hold your breath for an extended period of time, you may experience strong emotions like fear, sadness, and anger. By learning to relax into them, you are able to work through them and will be better able to handle similar emotions when they come up in everyday life. In that sense, breath-holding can be an indicator of how well you respond to stress and the degree to which you are in balance. You can practice breath-holding safely at home. Do not practice breath-holding in water without an expert present because you can pass out and drown.

The potential positive effects of breathwork really are unlimited. Stig says that breathwork is a way not just to rewire the nervous system, but also to tune in to our hearts. Breathwork is a way to come home to ourselves and redefine who we are and what is possible. When we expand our breathing, he says, we begin to have bigger thoughts, aspirations, and goals. And in his experience, we can even awaken an entirely new level of consciousness.[39]

Nadi Shodhana Pranayama
or Alternate Nostril Breathing

Alternate Nostril Breathing Exercise

Set five minutes aside to experiment with alternative nostril breathing. It's an old yogic practice that will help you come back to your center by balancing the left and right hemispheres of your brain. You may find it a bit odd to alternate the nostril you breathe through but give it a go and see how you feel.

- To start, close off your right nostril with your finger and inhale deeply through your left nostril.
- At the peak of your inhalation, lift your finger, close off your left nostril, and then exhale smoothly through your right nostril.
- After a full exhalation, inhale through the right nostril while still keeping your left nostril closed.
- At the peak of your inhalation, lift your finger, close off the right nostril with your finger, and exhale smoothly through your left nostril.
- Make the length of your inhale similar to that of your exhale and continue alternating your breathing through each nostril for a few minutes. The longer you practice, the more stable your mind and your emotions become.
- After a few rounds, begin to breathe to the count of 4-4-8. Inhale through the left nostril on four, hold your breath on four, and exhale through the right nostril on eight. Then you repeat with the right nostril.
- If you find this easy, you can go further by holding your breath for longer.

Holotropic Breathwork

I have personally had a taste of how powerful breathwork can be beyond the day-to-day slow deep breathing exercises. For several months I was a member of an online breathwork group called *NeuroDynamic Breathwork™*. Through the online platform, we would meet several times a week to engage in an hour-long breathing experience while listening to a set of very dynamic and evocative songs.[40]

The practice we were taught is not about balancing or calming our nervous system with slow breaths. Instead, the practice is based on a deep and continuous pattern of breathing through the mouth at a slightly faster pace than normal. The goal of this full diaphragmatic breath without pauses is to help the breather disconnect from their thinking mind, get in touch with their intuition, release stuck emotions, and improve health and well-being.

The technique—often referred to as Holotropic Breathing—was first developed by psychiatrists Christina and Stanislav Grof in the 1970's to achieve altered states of consciousness without drugs. They used the process of deep self-exploration brought on by these altered states as a therapeutic tool for healing.

I really wasn't sure what to expect the first time I attended the online breathwork session. I was aware, however, that the method can stimulate a psychedelic experience and cause hallucinations similar to drugs like DMT. Incredible, but true! Lying down in the comfort of my home, equipped with an eye mask and big headphones, I followed the instructions to breathe deeper and faster to the sound of the music. To my surprise, something started to shift after five to ten minutes of full, deep breaths through my mouth. My thinking mind became quieter and I felt waves of deep emotions, visions, and insights roll over me.

In my mind's eye, I clearly saw the people in my life that I'm closest to. One by one they appeared and my heart opened. Feelings of intense love and connection flooded my entire being in a way that I have rarely experienced before. Everything made sense. I felt so at home and connected to each of them.

With tears in my eyes, I continued the deep rhythmic breathing. The music became more dramatic, and so did my mood and the impressions. I felt squeezed as if I was in a water slide, and to my amazement I sensed that it was a birth experience. My rational mind became the onlooker and didn't have time to process what was happening. Before I knew it, I saw myself as a new-born happy baby, lying on my back with my legs in the air. Initially I was giggling away, but I quickly became overwhelmed with emotions of sadness and fear.

The rest of the session continued with similar intensity. It was like being in an experiential cinema with images, sounds, emotions, and insights flashing up and coming to the fore. I was astonished at the depth and richness of my experiences with this type of breathwork. Afterwards, it took a little while to come back to my rational mind and make sense of the experience. I felt cleansed, grateful, and intrigued, but also emotionally drained. I knew I wanted to try it again, and although each subsequent breathwork session has given me a different experience, it's always been deeply cleansing and insightful.

CHAPTER 5:

Using Meditation to Connect to the Peacefulness of Your Heart

---

"Whatever techniques you practice, realize that the message of the heart becomes clearer when the mind is quiet. And in order to truly quiet the mind, we need to bring the head into alignment with the heart."
— *Doc Childre, HeartMath Institute*

Meditation is a term that covers a broad range of methods and techniques that involve relaxation, focus, and awareness. Meditation isn't just one thing or one particular method. Joseph Goldstein, co-founder of the Insight Meditation Society, says that the basic underlying essence of any meditation practice is the understanding that the mind can be trained.[41] It can be trained in a variety of ways to strengthen particular faculties, for instance by practicing loving-kindness meditation, mindfulness meditation, or mantra meditation.

Although the word meditate means to ponder or think deeply about something, the idea of meditation isn't actually to think. On the contrary, the purpose is to distance ourselves from the many thoughts that race around in our mind so that we can become less attached and more centered. When we meditate, we don't analyze our experience or thoughts and we also don't dwell on the past or the future. Instead, we practice staying in the present moment by focusing on the breath, a mantra, a sound, or an object. After a while, our thoughts, emotions, and sensory impressions become peripheral. During those moments, we're able to enter a state of greater insight, relaxation, and awareness.

There are many different forms of meditation and there are different reasons why you might want to practice. Meditation can help you relax, create a clear and focused mind, and find inner stillness. It can also help you foster awareness, inquire about who you truly are, and assist you in cultivating compassion and forgiveness. Depending on what form of meditation you engage in, you may at times narrow your attention, for instance by concentrating on your breath or by repeating a mantra. At other times, you may widen your attention, for instance by observing everything you experience, including your thoughts, emotions, sensations, and sounds.

Although you are likely to make use of a technique to still your mind, it's important not to think of meditation as another technique, or as a doing-activity. Eckhart Tolle, the best-selling author of *The Power of Now*, reminds us that meditation is really about being and realizing that you are a human being, not just a human doing things. When you meditate you put your doing-self aside and create time to just be and notice what is.

Mindfulness is slightly different to meditation, although there is a big overlap between the two. Mindfulness is being aware. It is noticing and paying attention to everything that is happening inside of you and around you, including thoughts, feelings, sensations, sounds, imaginations, and behaviors. As you notice what is going on, you don't analyze what you are seeing, hearing, thinking, or feeling. You simply observe what is happening in a non-judgmental way.

For instance, if you hear a door slam, you're not trying to determine if it's a good sound or a bad sound or where it's coming from. It is simply a sound that you take note of. Similarly, when a thought pops into your mind, telling you that you are not a skilled meditator, or that you didn't handle a conversation with your co-worker very well, you see it for what it is—just a thought. You don't let it take over and you don't get possessed by it. You notice it and practice not getting emotionally involved with it. You can learn to be non-reactive to your own thoughts.

Mindfulness is incredibly powerful because it raises your general level of awareness. Instead of being reactive and on autopilot, you become more conscious and begin to have more choice over which thoughts, emotions, and behaviors you engage with. When you're on autopilot, you're effectively running your unconscious programs. It's when you become mindful and aware of your thought-patterns and programming that you can change them.

Mindfulness can be applied to any situation throughout the day. For instance, you can practice mindfulness while sitting in traffic, doing the dishes, walking the dog, or sitting in a meeting. Meditation is usually practiced for a specific amount of time when you can find a few minutes of solitude. You make use of mindfulness in most kinds of meditation because a high level of awareness is a key element of meditation. The opposite isn't necessarily true. You don't always meditate when you are being mindful. When you wash the dishes, for instance, and fully notice the temperature of the water, the smells, the sounds, and sensations of soaping and rinsing the dishes, it might feel meditative, but you are practicing mindfulness, not meditation.

The same could be said if you're discussing conflicting viewpoints with your team. If you apply mindfulness to that situation, it means you are staying fully present and observing what is going on outside of you as well as inside. You notice what is being said, how it's being said, how your co-workers are behaving, and how they might be feeling. At the same time, you notice your own thoughts, feelings, behaviors, and the physical sensations in your body. You are practicing mindfulness and being aware, but you are not meditating.

Many mistakenly believe that the goal of mindfulness and meditation is to get rid of thoughts and to stop them. That's mostly not the case. The mind is designed to think and it will, with few exceptions, continue to do so. In meditation, you practice not getting involved with thoughts and letting them pass by without getting caught up in them.

You can picture meditation as a practice of sitting at a bus stop with a constant stream of buses passing by. Each bus represents a thought. Before you know it, and without even realizing it, you're on one of those buses, excited to be going somewhere. When you meditate and you unintentionally jump on a bus, it's not wrong. It happens all the time. But as soon as you realize that you have got involved with a thought, you gently come back to the present moment. You get off the bus, find the bench, and practice simply sitting there, witnessing the traffic go by. There will always be traffic, so the goal of meditation is not to get rid of thoughts. The goal is to learn to allow your thoughts to drive on by without your attention or focus drifting away with them.

As you practice stilling your mind, you may become impatient and even be tempted to give up. It can be very hard to stop engaging with the many thoughts, problems, and images in your head. That's normal. The more you try, the harder it can actually be. One of the techniques that can help you drop into yourself is to use your senses and notice what is going on around you. The more you use your senses to connect to the present moment, the less you will be preoccupied with your thoughts.

Using the analogy of the bus stop, as you're sitting on the bench trying to watch the buses pass by, feel the air as it touches your skin. Notice your feet on the ground and feel the support of the bench you are sitting on. Listen to the traffic and the footsteps of people passing by. Notice the many shapes and colors in your environment and pay attention to the smells. There is no need to judge or analyze what you see, hear, feel, or smell. Just let the sensory inputs pass through you.

I know I make it sound very easy, but in reality, it's not easy at all. The mind will keep getting engaged with thoughts. The practice is about accepting whatever thoughts or feelings come up and gently bringing your attention back to the present moment. Whatever arises, allow it to be there. Accept the sounds and sensations. Accept your thoughts and feelings. Accept yourself just the way you are. And accept this moment just the way it is. There is no need to strive for anything. Don't even try to meditate. Just rest in the moment.

Being in the Present Moment Exercise

I invite you to spend five minutes practicing being fully present. When you're fully present and focus your attention on the sensations in your body, there is less space for rumination and thoughts. You give your busy thinking-mind something else to do. It stays in the here and now rather than engaging with past memories, limiting thoughts, or worrying about the future.

- Begin to notice how your body is feeling right at this moment. Tune in to each body part and notice the sensations that are present. Do you feel discomfort anywhere? Do you feel tingling sensations or tension in any part of your body?
- Notice your toes. Can you become sensitive to each individual toe, one by one?
- Now notice your legs. Connect with your shins, calves, knees, and thighs one by one. Notice how each part feels.
- Then move to your abdomen and chest. How do these parts of your body feel right now? Can you feel the heat in your belly? And can you notice your heartbeat?
- Then observe your breathing. Don't change it. Just pay attention to where you feel your breath entering and exiting your body and how your diaphragm is moving with it.

How did you find this little experiment? What did you notice? Did your mind wander or were you able to stay present with the sensations of your body?

The Benefits of Meditation

No matter how you choose to practice, meditation can help you feel more centered and get better at embracing the challenges of everyday life. That's because you begin to create some distance between what is happening inside of you and what is happening around you. Rather than identifying with and being controlled by your thoughts, feelings, impulses, and impressions, you take a step back from it all and become less entangled. You become better able to simply notice and accept what is happening right now in this moment without automatically getting sucked into any emotional drama. In other words, you become less reactive.

For example, imagine a co-worker confiding in you that she's having a really challenging time. She feels like an imposter, fears that she might lose her job, and she just had an argument with her husband. What would the effect of her story be on you? Think about it for a moment. Presumably you would sympathize or empathize with her. You would be supportive, listen to her, and help her understand the situation more clearly. But unless she's an extremely close friend, you probably wouldn't be consumed with her pain. You would be able to look at the situation objectively and consider what an appropriate response would be.

Now imagine for a moment that you are the one who feels like an imposter. You are the one who fears you might lose your job and you are the one who just had an argument with your partner. In this case you would most certainly feel the pain. You might even be out of your mind with worry. You might find it hard to focus and think clearly, and as a result you might say and do things reactively instead of making good decisions calmly and rationally.

Worrying about the events that happen in our life is an instinctive survival mechanism, which can motivate us to take action where action is due. But when we get too identified with our thoughts and emotions, we get sucked into the drama and lose the ability to perceive things objectively. It happens to all of us. We get possessed by fear and worry. We tense up, find it hard to sleep, and sometimes react in irrational ways. Wouldn't it be nice to create a bit of distance between the events that happen and your reactions? Wouldn't it be nice if you could be less tense, perceive the situation more objectively, and have more say in how you respond during challenging circumstances?

Mindfulness and meditation can help with that. They can help you quiet your mind and increase your awareness. You will find the more you practice, the more you become a conscious observer of your thoughts and feelings instead of being controlled by them. You begin to look at your thoughts and emotions from the outside like a friend would.[42] It's not an overnight fix, but over time you will definitely notice changes.

As your awareness grows, you will come to see that you are much more than a product of what you think, feel, say, and do. You will sense that your biggest power doesn't come from your thinking-mind. It comes from a deep place of stillness and inner wisdom. This is the seat of your soul. As Eckhart Tolle writes, "You are never more essentially, more deeply, yourself than when you are still."[43]

When you access this place of stillness, even if just for a brief moment, it can feel very liberating, joyful, and peaceful. From this place, you might receive an insight that helps you make an important decision, or you might spontaneously get a feeling that everything makes sense, and that you are deeply connected to everything. There is nothing religious or mystical about it. Accessing the stillness of your true self is available to everyone. All it takes is the willingness to quiet your thinking-mind.

In one of his many books, the Indian mystic, Osho, writes: "All meditation techniques are to make you courageous, strong, adventurous, so that you can stop holding onto the surface and fall within yourself. That which looks like an Abyss, dark, bottomless, is the very ground of your being. Once you leave the surface, the periphery, you will be centered. This centering is the aim of meditation. Once you are centered you can move to the periphery but you will be totally different."[44]

Spiritual leaders and meditation teachers have for a long time claimed that mindfulness and meditation lead to reduced stress, greater physical healing, emotional wellbeing, steadiness of attention, improved focus, and increased self-awareness. Interestingly, these observations have now been studied and scientifically proven. Some of the positive effects of meditation, such as reduced stress and increased emotional wellbeing, can be felt almost immediately.

When you meditate and enter a state of restful alertness, you quiet down the fight-or-flight response and instead trigger your body's rest, digest, and recovery system. Your breathing deepens, your heart rate decreases, the production of stress hormones goes down, inflammation decreases, and immune system function improves.[45] When you meditate you effectively signal to the parasympathetic nervous system that it's safe to calm down and relax, thereby enabling your body to recover and come into balance.

At the same time as you quiet down the fight-or-flight response, you give your thinking-mind a break. You shift your attention away from your busy mind and anxious thoughts and get in touch with a deeper, wiser, more quiet part of yourself. Over time, this practice allows your brain to develop new pathways beyond the worrying and anxious thoughts. The more you practice, the steadier and more centered you become. You will be better able to maintain your equilibrium and navigate when external events change.

The effects of meditation on your brain can be observed within weeks of starting a daily practice. In one study at Massachusetts General Hospital, researchers took images of the brain structure before and after an eight-week Mindfulness-Based Stress Reduction (MBSR) Program.[46] They found increased grey-matter density in the hippocampus, a part of the brain that is important for learning and memory. They also found increased grey-matter in brain structures associated with self-awareness, compassion, and introspection. Finally, grey-matter had decreased in the amygdala, which plays a central role in anxiety and stress. These changes in the brain aren't necessarily permanent if you stop meditation, but with regular practice they can be sustained and increased.

Many other studies have been carried out on the effects of MBSR, showing reduced levels of emotional exhaustion, psychological distress, depression, and anxiety. They also showed improvements in personal accomplishment, self-compassion, quality of sleep, and relaxation.[47] It's not surprising that stress, anxiety, and emotional wellbeing come up as significant benefits of mindfulness-based mediations as these practices are centered around observing your thoughts from a distance and accepting difficult emotions without getting sucked into them.

Transcendental Meditation (TM) is another well-known meditation technique that has been widely researched. It was developed by Maharishi Mahesh Yogi in India in the 50's based on ancient meditative yoga practices. It subsequently gained popularity in the West, attracting the attention of the Beatles and other celebrities. Several studies show that it is effective in reducing stress and anxiety, improving brain function, and lowering blood pressure.[48]

To practice this kind of meditation, sit with your eyes closed and silently repeat a mantra for 15-20 minutes twice a day.[49] By focusing on the mantra (such as "om") you quiet the thinking brain, transcend your thoughts, and reach a point of expansive silence. TM is taught by certified teachers all over the world through a standard course of instruction.

There are many ways to help you quiet your mind and make it easier to drop into that place of inner wisdom. There really isn't any right or wrong way as long as you practice staying present, relaxing your body, and letting go of your thoughts. Some people find that being physically active and practicing walking meditation, Tai Chi, Qigong, or Yoga puts their mind at rest. For others, breathing exercises are a great way to prepare for deeper forms of meditation.

From my own experience, focusing on my breath and paying attention to the sensations in my body is a great gateway to mindfulness and developing a deeper meditation practice. I find that when I focus on my body—and on my heart-center in particular—it moves my attention away from my busy mind toward a place of warmth and stillness within. I feel an almost instantaneous shift when I drop my attention from my head to my heart.

Connecting to Your Heart

I first became aware of the importance of consciously feeling my heart when I bought a meditation book decades ago. I felt stressed and exhausted and went to one of London's biggest bookstores in the hope of finding something profound. As I was looking through the self-help section, a book titled *Meditation for Busy People* by Osho jumped out. I felt it was speaking directly to me. I was busy. I didn't have much time to meditate, but I badly needed it.

The book was full of wisdom and exactly what I needed at the time. I read it several times and each time it helped me slow down and drop further into myself. I was particularly fascinated by the absurdity of simply sitting and watching the grass grow. In the book the author writes, "This is the very essence of meditation—sitting silently … doing nothing … the spring comes … and the grass grows by itself … Everything happens! You are not to be the doer."[50]

The book also helped me connect to my heart-center. I realized I had spent almost all of my time in my thinking brain. Osho reminded me that the heart is the source of peace. Whenever we feel peaceful, it's not something we are making up. Peace is coming from the heart, he says.[51] When we focus our attention on the heart-space, we are simply becoming aware of the source of peace that is always there. Whenever you bring your attention to your chest and consciously relax it, great peace will come. Your heart has become harmonious. All you needed to do was relax.

Over time, as you begin to shift your awareness from your head to your heart, you may notice things you didn't notice before. You may also find that people begin to respond to you differently. As you feel more peaceful within, the world becomes more peaceful toward you. It's fascinating! What you think and feel on the inside can transform how you perceive and experience what's happening on the outside.

Connecting to Your Heart Exercise

It's time for your next exercise on the journey of homecoming. Here I invite you to set aside ten minutes to drop into your heart-space and notice the peace that is already there. By engaging in this little exercise, you may feel a calming effect straight away or you may find it a little harder to access the peacefulness within. It took me a little while to feel something, so don't worry if it doesn't happen right away.

Step 1: Simply sit in a comfortable position and take some deep, relaxing breaths. Drop your shoulders and soften the small muscles in your face. Let your cheeks be heavy and let your jaw drop. Lower your gaze or close your eyes.

Step 2: Start to become aware of the area in between your two armpits. Tune in to this area in your chest with your full awareness and feel how it begins to soften and relax. With each exhalation, let go of tension and allow yourself to become more relaxed.

Step 3: Place your hands on your chest and feel the physical movement of your heart. Let it be a gesture of showing support for yourself and connecting with a deeper part of you. Notice a subtle expansion around your heart as you breathe in and a softening as you breathe out.

Step 4: Imagine that you are breathing directly in and out of your heart. The breath enters right in the middle of your chest and brings with it a warm and calming sensation. Stay here for a few minutes.

Step 5: Continue to breathe directly in and out of your heart-center and begin to notice a deep sense of peace emanating from it. It's like a blossoming flower, gradually opening up in the middle of your chest and displaying its beautiful petals. Can you feel the peace in your heart as you relax?

Step 6: Remain in this place of great relaxation and peace for as long as you need. Then open your eyes and let the feeling stay with you.

How did this practice make you feel? Perhaps the world around you seems a bit more distant now. Or perhaps you feel more centered in your own being. If you feel more peaceful, this is not something you're imagining. You are simply becoming aware of the source of peace that is always there within you.

The Science of the Heart

The deep feelings of calm and connectedness that we experience when we tune in to our heart have been studied scientifically for a long time. Scientists at the pioneering research institute HeartMath have studied the psychophysiology of stress, emotions, and the interactions between the heart and the brain for over 25 years.[52] What they found is that one of the most effective ways to reduce stress and feelings of being overwhelmed is to improve the quality of the signals that go from the heart to the brain.

Interestingly, the heart contains the strongest electrical and magnetic fields in the body, and it sends more neuro messages to the brain and to the nervous system than it receives from them.[53] In fact, the heart is about 60 times stronger electrically and 100 times stronger magnetically than the brain.[54]

HeartMath's research has shown that different patterns of heart activity, which correspond to different emotional states, have distinct effects on the brain.[55] Uplifting emotions, such as appreciation, joy, care, and love produce an ordered and stable pattern of the heart's input to the brain. This coherent heart rhythm pattern improves your physical, mental, and emotion wellbeing. When you enter a state of coherence, your physiological systems function more efficiently, you experience greater emotional stability, and you also have increased mental clarity, attention, and improved cognitive function.[56] In addition, you are better able to access your creativity and deeper states of intuition.

In contrast, when you experience stress and negative emotions, the pattern of the heart rhythm is erratic, and the signals that travel from the heart to the brain inhibit higher cognitive and emotional functions. In other words, emotions such as anger, frustration, and anxiety result in an incoherent heart rhythm pattern, which limits your ability to think clearly, to remember, to learn, to reason, and to make effective decisions. An incoherent heart rhythm pattern also reinforces the emotional experience of stress.

This ground-breaking research confirms that, by accessing your heart and focusing on uplifting emotions of love, compassion, and gratefulness, not only will you feel more peaceful, but you will also have increased mental clarity and greater physical health. It's interesting how so many of the world's wisdom traditions encourage us to focus on feelings of love and gratitude in order to create better lives for ourselves and others. Now researchers are proving the science behind this wisdom.

In a recent documentary, the Dalai Lama said, "Scientists now say that constant fear, anger, and hatred is eating our immune system. In the long run, these destructive emotions are very bad for our health and for our peace of mind. When fear, suspicion, anger, and jealousy are active in your mind, you never get genuine relaxation. On the other hand, emotions like warm-heartedness, sense of concern for others, bring inner strength and self-confidence. They are the basis of peace of mind."[57]

It turns out, there are two major ways for you to create a more coherent heart rhythm pattern. One of them is to breathe slowly and rhythmically at a ten to twelve second pattern. We discussed this Coherent Breathing practice in the previous chapter. You spend five or six seconds inhaling and five or six seconds exhaling, creating a smooth, circular breath, ideally of 5.5 breaths per minute. This kind of breath makes you feel calm, yet energized and responsive. This method alone can be transformational. I've shared it many times with my coaching clients, who find that it has an immediate centering effect on them.

The other way to come into coherence is to intentionally feel uplifting emotions such as appreciation, joy, love, and compassion. According to HeartMath, this is the more powerful way, because when you feel positive emotions your breathing rhythm automatically synchronizes with your heart, and thereby reinforces the positive state you are in. This in itself is a testimony to why it's beneficial to spend more time doing the things you love. When you spend time playing, walking in nature, connecting with friends, or being creative, your uplifting emotions will have an immediate and positive effect on your biochemistry.

Practicing Gratitude

According to scientists, a regular gratitude practice can have powerful effects on your mental, emotional, and physical health. Dr. Joe Dispenza writes that something as simple as moving into an elevated state of joy, love, or gratitude for five to ten minutes a day can produce significant epigenetic changes in our health and bodies.[58]

If you enjoy writing, you can put pen to paper and express your joy and appreciation that way. Many people habitually set aside a few minutes each day to journal and focus on something they appreciate and are grateful for. It doesn't have to be anything big or time-consuming. It can be feeling the heat of the sun, the presence of a pet, or a gesture of kindness from a stranger. When you bring to mind something you're grateful for, it's particularly powerful to focus on the richness of the situation and notice the sensations in your body. That means paying attention to any sounds, smells, tastes, visual impressions, and feelings that are present for you. Really savor the moment when you are practicing feeling these positive emotions.

A few days ago I met up with three female friends I don't get to see very often. We went to a small Japanese restaurant where they served excellent food and wine. It was a fun and joyful evening filled with laughter and deep conversations. Thinking back on it, I can hear the sounds from the restaurant, taste the delicious teriyaki salmon, and feel the warmth in my heart. Focusing on the sensations in my body brings back a feeling of gratefulness and I notice my breathing automatically becomes more coherent.

If you're going through a tough time at the moment and find it hard to appreciate anything, consider that your breath is always there no matter who you are, working for you and doing its magic. You mostly take it for granted but you wouldn't be here without it. Spending a few moments appreciating your breath fully and noticing the feelings of love and gratitude in your body can have a profound effect on how you feel.

Neuroscientist and tenured professor at Stanford School of Medicine, Andrew Huberman, says that the neurological and anti-inflammatory impacts of a gratitude practice are on par with some of the effects of pharmacology and high intensity interval training. In fact, long lasting impacts can be obtained with the right kind of practice, if it's performed repeatedly for as little as once a week. People typically report feeling happier, more meaning, joy, and even awe for their life experience. In addition, studies show that a regular gratitude practice can benefit social relationships and provide resilience to trauma.[59]

According to Huberman, studies show that the most potent form of gratitude practice isn't necessarily one where you express gratitude, but one where you receive it. When someone expresses gratitude to you, it has the potential to profoundly shift your neurology more so than the neurology of the person who gives it.

To benefit from this kind of gratitude practice, you'd have to focus on a time when someone was thankful for something you did. This could be a time when someone thanked you for a gift you gave them, for paying them a visit, or for a donation you provided.

Just a few days ago one of my connections on LinkedIn sent me a private message to express her gratitude for a small video I posted. The video was about how to overcome low self-esteem. It turned out that she had gone through an intense period at work with more projects coming in than she could comfortably handle. She described her feelings of being overwhelmed and how my video had helped her "put a different thinking cap on."

As I bring to mind how appreciative she was, it brings warmth to the core of my being and makes me feel that the work I do has meaning. It also makes me think of a time when an entire team in the Philippines had used my free YouTube videos to run a training course. They were sweet enough to send me a picture of them in front of a monitor where my video was playing. They were smiling and giving me the thumbs up. The photo is etched in my memory and still brings a joyful smile to my face whenever I think of it.

You might think reminiscing about memories like this is a waste of time, but research shows that the effects of this kind of intentional practice of feeling and receiving gratitude can be as powerful as a high intensity interval training workout.

Powerful Stories

Another potent way of tapping into the power of gratitude is to watch, read, or recall a story where someone else receives help in a positive way. Perhaps you can think of a story that's particularly meaningful to you and that moves you, for instance a story of survivors of genocide and how people helped them along the way. When you think of such a story, you're likely to identify with, and feel empathy for the main character and be moved by the help they received.

One such story that I find incredibly moving is Immaculée Ilibagiza's account of how she survived the atrocious 1994 genocide in Rwanda. At the age of 22, her world was ripped apart when her Tutsi family was brutally murdered during a killing spree that claimed the lives of nearly one million Rwandans. Remarkably, Immaculée survived the massacre when a local pastor from the Hutu ethnic group risked his life by hiding Immaculée along with seven other women in his home. Huddled silently together in a cramped bathroom, the women spent 91 days in fear that the machete-wielding killers would find them. The pastor told the members of his family, who didn't know the women had taken refuge in the house, that the key to the spare bathroom had gone missing. The hunters ransacked the house twice, but the pastor kept his cool and miraculously the door to the bathroom remained locked.

Immaculée is a great story-teller and has captured her remarkable story in her book, *Left to Tell*.[60] In the book she speaks about her strong faith and how she found strength in prayer and her unyielding relationship with God. She emerged from the bathroom hideout having discovered the meaning of an unconditional love so strong that she was able to shed her fear of death and forgive her family's killers. Listening to Immaculée's story, it's evident that circumstances can bring out the worst in people but they certainly can also bring out the best. It fills my heart with hope and gratitude to know that even amidst darkness and evil, miracles do happen. What's more, shortly after Immaculée arrived in the US she met best-selling author Wayne Dyer at a seminar and he agreed to publish her book.

Another story that springs to mind is when Tony Robbins experienced one of the most challenging and powerful moments of his life. It was Thanksgiving, Tony was 11 years old, and his family didn't have any money or food. His mom and dad were fighting like cats and dogs, saying things that once you say them you can never take back. His mom screamed at his father, proclaiming that he couldn't even take care of his own family. Then, a miracle happened!

Someone knocked on the door, and when Tony opened it, he found a stranger with a huge box of food as a present for the family. Next to him on the ground was a black pot with an uncooked turkey in it. Seeing it as a gift from God, Tony was beside himself with joy and gratitude. He went to get his father and couldn't wait to see the smile on his face. But his father saw the situation very differently. He was resentful and agitated and didn't want to take the food. He felt defeated and inadequate. Eventually, he gave in and reluctantly accepted the gift. But sadly, Tony's father ended up leaving the family shortly after because he felt worthless and hadn't been able to feed his family.

At the time, this was the worst and most crushing experience of Tony's life. But, in spite of his pain, his life took a new and different trajectory. The fact that a stranger had turned up with food gave him the belief that strangers care. And, if strangers cared about him and his family, he decided he was going to care about strangers. This insight changed his life. He promised himself that one day he would do well enough to do the same thing for other families.

Tony didn't wait until he became wealthy to provide for others. When he was 17, he had a car and a bit of money, and when Thanksgiving arrived, he decided to feed two families in need. He went on the biggest shopping spree of his life, buying enough food for two or three days for each family. Disguised as a delivery boy, he drove to the first family with bags of groceries and a note saying: *This is a gift from a friend. Please know that you are loved. I want you to have an extraordinary Thanksgiving. You deserve it! Please accept this gift.*

He knocked on the door and a small Hispanic woman appeared on the other side. She was so ecstatic that she let out a scream when she saw all the food. She started kissing Tony all over and was moved to tears as she read the note. It turned out she had five children and her husband had left her three days prior with no money or food. As she and her children waved goodbye, she was crying hysterically and smiling from ear to ear.

In that moment Tony realized that the worst day of his life had been the best day of his life because, if his father had not walked out, he would not have had that experience. Because of what happened when he was 11, he had built a new life with the desire and drive to give back to others. The following year Tony fed four families, and the year after that he fed eight.[61] He continued to double his efforts, and in the last five years, The Tony Robbins foundation fed 525 million meals to those in need.[62] I still get tears in my eyes whenever I hear this story.

Appreciation and Gratefulness Exercise

Set aside five minutes to think about a positive experience you've had recently that makes you feel appreciation. Engaging in this kind of gratitude practice can profoundly shift your biochemistry and benefit your mental, emotional, and physical health.

- Think of a recent event that made you feel warm and appreciative. It doesn't have to be anything big. It could be hearing from a friend you haven't heard from for a while. It could be a stranger smiling at you on the street, watching the sunrise on your morning commute, or the tree outside your window.
- Let the feelings of gratefulness and appreciation fill your entire body. Don't just think about it. Really feel the feelings of love and warmth in your body.
- As you inhale, open your heart and breathe in gratitude. As you exhale slowly, breathe out love into the world.
- Stay here for a few minutes, receiving and offering and tasting each breath.
- Now think about the last time someone expressed gratitude to you, even if it was just a small gesture. Perhaps they thanked you for your presence, for your time, for a favor, or for a gift you gave them.
- How did you feel when you received that person's gratitude? Fully step into those feelings and re-experience them now. Then spend a few minutes capturing the experience on paper in as much detail as you can.

We know from science that a regular gratitude practice can have powerful effects on your overall health and happiness. Why not turn this into a daily ritual?

Emotional Blockages

For some people it's relatively easy to feel gratefulness, compassion, and appreciation and to connect to the heart-center. If you find it difficult to feel warmth or peacefulness when you focus on your heart-center, perhaps you're used to operating in a more head-based mode. Perhaps you're a busy and driven person and tend to rely on your rational mind to move forward. You enjoy getting things done and perhaps you even feel guilty when you attempt to relax your thinking and drop into yourself. After all, there is so much on your to-do-list.

If this rings true for you, don't worry. Whenever you're stuck in traffic, waiting in line, or find yourself in between one do-ing activity and the next, resist the temptation to reach for your phone and make yourself busy. These are magical moments that you can use to switch from a head-based doing mode to a heart-based being mode. Use these moments to be still, to breathe deeply, and to drop into your heart. The more you practice the easier it becomes.

Another reason you might find it challenging to connect to your heart-center is that there may be an emotional block in your way. Perhaps you experience deep feelings of anger, fear, or sadness. Or perhaps you are extremely self-critical and find it difficult to show kindness toward yourself. As we discussed in chapter one, this is a common pattern. Unfortunately, many people believe that they are not good enough and are not worthy of love. Whenever they make a mistake, they use it against themselves to prove that they once again are not worthy. It's very hard to witness someone denying themselves the kind of self-love and self-care we all need and deserve.

You may have gotten the impression that you should suppress negative emotions and favor positive ones to create inner peace and a coherent heart rhythm pattern. But it's not as simple as that. Strong feelings of anger, fear, depression, or self-hatred only hold you back when you try to avoid them and sweep them under the carpet. You need to consciously see, feel, hear, and accept your emotions to release them properly. Attempting to avoid painful emotions or experiences by only focusing on positive or pleasant experiences is called spiritual bypassing. If you only want to entertain the pleasant parts of your mind and suppress what is unpleasant, you are not doing the inner work. In fact, that's just avoiding the work.

Meditation and gratefulness practices should never be a substitute for addressing deeper traumas and emotional blockages. Meditation is not about going somewhere happy in your mind to escape reality. It's about observing what is going on inside of you—no matter what emerges—and bringing compassion to your experience. Sometimes that will lead you to very positive feelings while other times you will experience very powerful and painful feelings which need to be experienced and released. If you suppress your feelings, they will eventually bubble up and make themselves heard in undesirable and uncontrollable ways.

If you have a deeply-rooted belief that you are not good enough, or if you're struggling with a trauma, you might want to consider working with a therapist. Even if it's upsetting to work through trauma, it's essential to get to the bottom of it so that it doesn't end up controlling you and consuming you. Meditation works well in conjunction with therapy and other healing modalities as a tool to increase your awareness of your inner landscape. It can help you feel unconditional love and compassion for yourself. It can also help you accept, forgive, and free yourself from the past by making peace with the gremlins of your mind. In the next chapter, we will examine more closely how to do that.

Loving-Kindness Meditation

Let's explore the classic meditation practice of loving-kindness. This type of meditation can help you more deeply connect with your heart by cultivating feelings of love and compassion toward yourself and others. Not only is the loving-kindness meditation a good way to open your heart, it also helps create coherence by generating uplifting emotions and slowing down your breathing.

Loving-kindness meditation is one of the best ways to generate an attitude of compassion toward people with whom you have difficulties. It can also help you feel more compassion for yourself and for situations or experiences that have been very stressful or difficult for you. If you feel anger, fear, or resentment toward someone or something, loving-kindness meditation will be a great practice for you to explore. This practice is one of the most well-studied meditation techniques and it has been linked to reduced levels of depression, anxiety, and post-traumatic stress.

Dr. Barbara Fredrickson and Dr. Richard Davidson are among the researchers who have extensively studied this kind of meditation.[63] Dr. Fredrickson and her team concluded that the practice led to shifts in people's daily experiences of positive emotions such as love, joy, and gratitude. Over the course of nine weeks, these shifts were linked to an increase in self-acceptance, positive relationships with others, and good physical health.

Dr. Richard Davidson is the founder of the Center for Healthy Minds at the University of Wisconsin-Madison. When he studied the brain of long-term practitioners of loving-kindness meditations, he found increased activation of the parts of the brain that are responsible for our ability to empathize and attune to the emotional states of others.[64] Both long-term meditators and beginners experienced higher levels of compassion, but long-term meditators showed significantly more activation in the part of the brain associated with empathy.

The Dalai Lama, who has collaborated with Dr. Richardson since the 90's, was right when he said that emotions like warm-heartedness and sense of concern for others bring inner strength and self-confidence.[65] In fact he was the driving force behind Dr. Richardson's initial research into this area, challenging him to study the positive effects of kindness and compassion training.[66]

The Dalai Lama says that "people get the impression that the practice of love, forgiveness, and altruism is good for others and not necessarily themselves. That's totally wrong. When we practice love and compassion, the benefit firstly goes to the person who practices it. Then through that action other people may benefit too. As you practice, you immediately get a calmer and more peaceful mind. It also gives you more inner strength, more self-confidence. Altruism is the best way to fulfill your own happiness."[67]

It's worth bearing in mind, that altruistic behavior shouldn't be motivated by a feeling of guilt or obligation. If you feel like you have to give to others while neglecting your own fundamental needs, it indicates an unhealthy pattern, which could leave you burned out or resentful. True altruism comes from a deep place of feeling that you have love to give to others, not because you feel obligated to help, but because you deeply want to. With these caveats in mind, shifting your focus away from yourself and toward others, can have a profound impact on your emotional wellbeing.

A few years ago, several of my friends were going through a difficult time. One was in intensive care with the COVID virus and another had just been diagnosed with cancer and was undergoing treatment. A third friend was heart-broken after just one year in a marriage that broke down. I often held them in my thoughts during my meditations and visualized sending them love, light, and healing energy. I don't know if my positive emotions had any effect on their recovery, but there is no doubt that the practice helped me cultivate my own feelings of compassion, and that it made me feel closer and more connected to them and to myself.

Loving-Kindness Meditation Exercise

Please allocate ten minutes for this next exercise. It's a beautiful practice that will help you open your heart and cultivate compassion toward yourself and others.

Step 1: Start with a few minutes of breathing mindfully while inhaling and exhaling a little deeper and slower than usual. Sit quietly and allow yourself to relax.

Step 2: Imagine a gentle shower of golden light trickling down over the top of your head and radiating throughout your body. As this beam of golden light travels through every part of your body, and through your heart, allow yourself to let go of any tension. Give yourself permission to be fully relaxed.

Step 3: Bring your awareness to your heart area and consciously relax it. Stay in this place and notice a big, warm sensation of peace in the middle of your chest.

Step 4: As you sense your heart opening up, visualize being kind and loving to yourself in whichever way comes most natural to you. Perhaps you're hugging yourself, comforting yourself, or simply seeing yourself fully. Then silently repeat any of the following phrases: *May I be well. May I be happy. May I be safe and free from suffering.*

Step 5: If there is no one around to physically hug you, why not give yourself a big hug by wrapping your arms around your chest? It's completely fine to feel emotional. If tears flow, let them flow. Stay in this moment for as long as you need.

Step 6: Prepare yourself to move on to the next stage of the meditation, where you bring to mind a good friend you feel positively connected to. Perhaps your friend is going through a difficult time at the moment and would benefit from your loving thoughts. If you can't think of a friend, it's perfectly okay to bring to mind your pet or someone from your past.

Step 7: Imagine your friend in your mind's eye and feel your heart open toward them. Repeat the phrases: *May you be well. May you be happy. May you be safe and free from suffering.*

Step 8: As you think about them, you may find it useful to imagine your own light radiating and reaching them wherever they are. You can visualize this as the gentle shower of golden light flowing through you and into your friend as you hold hands.

Step 9: In the next phase of the meditation, bring to mind a neutral person or a stranger and send them wishes of love and kindness. This can be someone you passed on the street this morning or someone who served you at the local shop. It can be anyone you have no assumptions about and feel neutral toward. Open your heart to this stranger and repeat the phrases: *May you be well. May you be happy. May you be safe and free from suffering.*

Step 10: Now that your heart is opening up more fully, bring to mind a person with whom you have difficulty at the moment. It can be anyone who you feel conflicted toward; a colleague, a family member, a neighbor, or a politician. Make a real effort to open your heart to them and wish them well. If you feel resistance, that's okay. Accept that this is how you are currently feeling about them. Take a deep breath in and repeat the phrases: *May you be well. May you be happy. May you be safe and free from suffering.*

Step 11: The final stage of the meditation is to gradually widen your awareness and give love and kindness to all living beings. Start small by first sending love and kindness to your inner circle of family and friends, and to your local community. Repeat the phrases: *May you be well. May you be happy. May you be safe and free from suffering.*

Step 12: Gradually widen the circle to your city, your country, and eventually to the entire planet. Let your heart go out to all sentient beings, including insects, fish, birds, and trees. Hold the natural world and the entire planet in your awareness and repeat the phrases: *May you be well. May you be happy. May you be safe and free from suffering.* Reconnect with that big, bright star in the middle of your chest and see how your light reaches and encompasses the entire planet.

How was this exercise for you? Did you find any of the steps particularly pleasant or challenging? If you found it difficult to send loving thoughts to yourself, that's okay. Simply notice it. Resist the temptation to go down a rabbit hole of feeling shame or guilt. You are practicing opening up your heart and becoming aware of what is happening inside of you. Awareness is good, just don't use it as a stick to beat yourself up with. Be gentle with yourself no matter what emerges.

CHAPTER 6:

Befriending Your Challenging Thoughts and Emotions

"We must be willing to encounter darkness and despair when they come up and face them, over and over again if need be, without running away or numbing ourselves in the thousands of ways we conjure up to avoid the unavoidable."
—*Jon Kabat-Zinn*

When everything is going well and you feel good, it's easier to sit still and drop into your heart-center. But when strong feelings of anger, sadness, fear, grief, or shame are present, it's much more challenging because you're being hijacked by your emotional brain. When you finally decide to sit down and be still, difficult memories and emotions may crop up for no apparent reason.

It's also possible that strong emotions crop up because of something that's happened to you recently. You may keep replaying a past event in your mind. Perhaps you have thoughts like, *I can't believe he said that to me. I'm being treated so unfairly. It makes me feel angry and worthless.* When you continually go back to a past situation that was upsetting, it makes your strong emotions flare up, again and again. In your mind, you may find yourself trying to justify your actions or place blame. That's very understandable, but to find peace you will need to practice another way of being. Justifying, blaming someone else, or denying a situation will never resolve the situation or your emotions. The nagging feeling will remain because you haven't been fully present with it. You haven't fully released it.

Emotions want to be accepted and acknowledged. When you acknowledge an emotion—by openly experiencing it and befriending it—it loosens its grip on you because it's being heard. That's why you need to turn toward an emotion, even if it seems counterintuitive to face that which is scary. Avoiding emotions only makes them worse over time. The emotion you ignore and push down will resurface at a later stage. What you resist persists until you find a better way.

You may think you are facing the unpleasant emotion by replaying the upsetting scenario over and over in your mind or by telling yourself how unfairly you have been treated. But in this case, you're simply retriggering your inbuilt fight-or-flight response. When you keep thinking about the situation, the unpleasant emotion comes up again and again, but it's not being released. A better way of responding would be to take a step back and observe what's going on in your mind and body. Rather than being sucked into the drama, become an objective observer. You can do that by being open and curious about where your strong emotions are coming from and what the thought-patterns are that have triggered them.

Self-inquiry can be painful because it brings up deep emotions and memories from the past that can be difficult to digest. That's why many of us have a tendency to turn our back on challenging emotions. It seems easier to avoid them than face those painful and scary feelings. But self-inquiry and curiosity about our reactions and emotional triggers is an important part of the inner journey.

While working with John, one of my coaching clients, he told me that whenever he walked into the offices in the morning he'd almost instantly feel down because no one was saying good morning to him. The voice in his mind kept saying, *My bosses aren't looking up and saying good morning when I arrive. It's because I'm a nobody. They don't value me and I'm not doing a good enough job.* He kept telling himself this story over and over throughout the day to the point where it affected his confidence and his concentration levels. It made him feel sad and worthless. John was unconsciously feeding a story that he'd been telling himself his entire life. It's the common self-limiting belief of I'm not good enough. Growing up in a large family, John never felt seen or accepted by his mother. He was constantly seeking her love and attention by going after bigger and bigger accomplishments in life, but nothing was ever good enough to fill that void inside him.

I invited John to sit with the sadness and feel the feelings of not being good enough. There was no talking involved in this step. He simply sat with the unpleasantness and felt the sadness of not being good enough. Of course, it was painful for him to connect with his old wound. But the only way out is through. By allowing himself to fully experience the unpleasant feelings of not being good enough, he began to expand into them, to make friends with them, and to gradually free himself from them.

He realized that he could experience the feelings without being consumed or feeling overwhelmed by them. By enduring the experience, he began to take back control because he was no longer afraid of his feelings. Through this experience he also came to understand that his bosses and colleagues weren't deliberately ignoring him or trying to put him down. He had simply allowed their actions to feed his self-limiting narrative and insecurities.

How to Release Emotions

You need to stop the mind chatter, sit still, and feel those painful or scary emotions so that you can make friends with them. Breathe slowly and deeply as you become fully present with how you are feeling. Allow whichever emotions come up to simply be there. Instead of avoiding them, try to relax into them. Experience these feelings fully and see them for what they are without running away. Sit with the disappointment, anger, guilt, fear, grief, and sadness without rejecting them.

Eventually you will get to the point where the emotions begin to loosen their grip on you. They have been heard and they have run their course. Remember, no matter how painful or scary an emotional experience is, it will always come to an end. Sometimes we get so swept up in emotion that it feels like it will always feel this bad or that things will never get better, but every emotional experience is only temporary. By allowing your emotions to be felt and run their course, you are finally creating space to let them go and heal.

Initially, it can be really hard to allow yourself to feel these emotions, let alone make friends with them. That's why they have the power to control you, and that's why you sometimes push them away, blame others, overanalyze, distract yourself, work too much, shop too much, or drink too much. But fully feeling an emotion won't destroy you or make it last forever. The emotion will run its course and dissipate once it's been heard.

When the emotion dies down you will be able to think more clearly and be free to act consciously rather than reacting based on an emotional trigger. My therapist used to say that real freedom is when you are conscious enough of what's going on inside of you to actively choose how to respond to a situation. If you're possessed by an emotion that you don't want to feel, the emotion is effectively dictating your actions. By increasing your awareness you increase your freedom.

An emotion I often struggle with is vulnerability. Feeling vulnerable can be scary and overwhelming, so whenever a situation arises that makes me feel that way, I automatically resort to strategies that help me avoid it. I become defensive, express anger, or hide in my work. Work is a favorite go-to strategy because it makes me feel the exact opposite: independent, strong, and worthy.

Sometimes I think, *If I can just accomplish enough at work, I won't ever have to feel so vulnerable again.* But hiding from the emotion is not healthy. By hiding from my vulnerability, I'm closing the door to the gremlin, and allowing it to unconsciously control me. As long as I keep the door closed, the gremlin will keep knocking. Whenever that feeling of vulnerability knocks, I feel tension and I use one of my many strategies to avoid it. But the more I resist, the more it persists, and the more I find myself stuck in an unhealthy pattern of behavior. What's more, all these pent-up emotions and disappointments that I avoided over the years get stored in my body where they create stress and dis-ease.

We all have patterns like this where we resort to some kind of defense mechanism to protect us from feelings that, in the past, seemed too big and scary to fully feel. But avoiding the negative emotions is not healthy. It is a form of self-rejection, self-denial, and self-sabotage.

Feeling into your emotional pain is uncomfortable so it's understandable that you want to avoid it. But you don't resolve anything by avoiding it and you end up making things worse. If you don't allow yourself to feel your feelings of fear, anger, or darkness, they can come out in uncontrollable behaviors, anxiety, panic attacks, and even disease and pain in your body.

Similarly, you won't be able to process your emotional pain by staying in your head and analyzing, blaming, or justifying the situation. You can think all you want about how angry someone made you, but this thought process won't free you or release your anger. Releasing emotional pain requires you to be present with how you really feel, rather than automatically avoiding your emotions or using your intellect to think about the situation over and over. You cannot resolve your feelings of anger, sadness, or hurt with your mind. This is why you have to use your heart so you can release these painful emotions and heal.

How do you begin to take deep feelings of anger, sadness, and hurt and hold them with acceptance and self-compassion?

How do you begin to bring healing to your vulnerability? Mindfulness, breathwork, coaching, therapy, mind-body practices, and the exercises in this book are all great tools that can help you do that.

To heal and come home to yourself, you have to address your difficulties with care, compassion, and acceptance. A trusted friend or therapist can point you in the right direction but they cannot do the work for you. They can support you and guide you and help you feel safe, but they cannot befriend those emotions for you. They cannot release the physical tension that you are holding in your body. You are the only one who can do that. Until you open the door and face your gremlins, they will continue to cause disturbances in your life.

The first step to healing is becoming aware of your patterns. By shining the spotlight of your awareness on your thoughts, emotions, and behaviors, you can begin to accept the patterns and the feelings. As we have seen in previous chapters, meditation and breathwork can both help with this process. They can help you become more aware and observe what is going on inside of you while regulating your nervous system. They can also help you feel grounded and more compassionate toward yourself. Meditation and breathwork are also great practices to use alongside coaching or therapy. Remember, healing takes time so don't give up if you don't get instant results the first time you meditate or breathe deeply.

If you're not sure what to do, simply begin to acknowledge how you are feeling in a given situation. Maybe you think to yourself, *I feel angry right now. Yes. And I feel sad and let down.* Meditation teacher and psychologist, Tara Brach, has written extensively about emotional healing. She says that saying "yes" to your emotions helps you to allow your emotions to be there without blaming anyone. It signals that you shouldn't feel bad about experiencing these emotions. Name whatever comes up. *Angry. Yes. Disappointed. Yes.*

By naming it, you recognize what is happening instead of avoiding or denying your feelings. Rather than being controlled by, in denial of, or hiding from the emotion, you become the observer who is fully aware and conscious of what is going on. If you've been in the habit of resisting your feelings, intellectualizing them, or pretending they don't exist, it may take time for you to allow yourself to really become aware of how you are feeling. That's okay. It's part of the healing process.

Once you name the emotion, you can gently turn toward it. With each in-breath, you can say, *Allow. Allow. Allow.* And with each out-breath you can say, *Soften. Soften. Soften.* You're not analyzing past scenarios in your mind and you're not trying to fix anything or blame anyone. You're simply sitting, relaxing, and allowing the emotions to be there. You breathe from deep within your abdomen and keep in mind that it's with each exhale that you release tension.

Whenever you engage in deep inner work and feel strong emotions rise up, remember to be kind and support yourself. Imagine yourself as a young child and treat yourself with the love, kindness, and tenderness that every young child deserves. Access that wise and compassionate part of you that instinctively knows how to be with a child. You would probably be kind and supportive and tell them that it's okay to feel the way they do. You most certainly wouldn't be shaming them, judging them, or denying the validity or reality of their emotions.[68] Give yourself the same support when facing difficult emotions that you would give a young child.

In such moments of tenderness and vulnerability, you can also call on your inner resources. You can imagine being supported and cared for by your circle of allies, ancestors, God, or anything or anyone else that makes you feel safe, strong, and grounded. In addition, you may find it helpful to say soothing phrases to yourself like:

- *This is a challenging moment for me. That's okay. Everybody experiences challenging moments. It's part of life.*
- *I'm going to be okay and I know that this too shall pass.*
- *I give myself the strength, support, and compassion I need to meet this situation.*
- *This is an opportunity to grow and free myself from the past.*

It's worth bearing in mind that feelings are neither good nor bad, and that you're not trying to change them or make them go away. The idea is to open up to them and make friends with them so they no longer impact you in the same negative way. When you do that, the emotions dissipate like clouds in the sky because they have been acknowledged. You are learning to make peace with your sadness, fear, anxiety, shame, hurt, and other powerful feelings.

Somatic Experiencing

If an emotion lingers for a while or you're unsure why it keeps coming back, it can be useful to notice in which part of your body it presents itself and what it looks like in terms of shape, size, texture, and color. Emotions can manifest in many ways. I've coached people who experienced their sadness as a dark, solid knot in the middle of their stomach or their anger as a red, hot fire in their throat. It's fascinating how the body stores our emotions.

You may notice that, as you observe your emotion, it begins to change its shape, size, or color. Feelings aren't fixed. They come and go and change when you observe them. The nature of feelings is to flow, and part of this journey is to simply learn to let your feelings flow without resisting them or trying to stop them. As you feel your feelings deeply, perhaps your emotion becomes brighter, smaller, and softer. Or maybe your emotion is beginning to loosen its grip on you because you are giving it space and allowing yourself to fully feel and see it.

You can also talk out loud or in your head to your emotions to find out if they have a message for you. There will be a reason why the emotion has shown up right at this moment. In one way or another, it's trying to serve you. It has a message for you. You can say, *Hi anger, can you tell me why you're here? What is it that I need to learn from you? What is it you're needing? What it is that I'm needing?*

Is it possible the emotion has your best interest at heart and is simply trying to protect you and look out for you? Put your arms around this vulnerable part of yourself and give it a hug. Be kind and gentle. Whisper soothing words of comfort, love, and forgiveness. Stay here for as long as you need. It's a tender moment. You're embracing a long-lost part of yourself.

I remember vividly the first time I came across this technique of locating an emotion in the body and feeling into it at a somatic level. It was at a Quantum Skills for Coaches workshop about fifteen years ago in central London, run by author and Leadership Coach, Annette Simmons.[69] At one point during the workshop, she asked for a volunteer who'd be willing to work through a strong emotion with her. A lady raised her hand and took a seat next to Annette in front of the audience.

Annette asked the volunteer to name her emotion and describe its size, color, shape, and texture. The lady described the intense pressure she was feeling. She said it felt like something was weighing her down. She went on to explain that this feeling manifested as two large steel rods sitting above both of her shoulders, pushing her down.

Annette continued to ask her to focus on the two steel rods and to describe the pressure, texture, color, and movement. To our amazement, the lady soon reported that the pressure seemed to decrease and that the rods were shrinking. At one point they completely lifted away from her shoulders and retracted. It was fascinating. By focusing on the emotion and how it manifested in her body, it seemed to have loosened its grip on her. I was just as surprised as the lady who volunteered.

Annette then asked the lady if she was able to communicate with the emotion. How did the emotion feel about being suppressed? What did the emotion want to say to her? At this point a conversation opened up with the emotion and tears were flowing from the lady's eyes as she allowed herself to feel what was really going on and listen to her own inner wisdom.

This is one of the most powerful techniques I've come across, and I continue to use it with my own clients. What you resist persists. Don't reject your emotions. Go into them and experience them. When you fully feel your feelings, you may initially get the impression that your pain is growing. That's because you're bringing something to the surface that was previously hidden from view. But as you continue to focus on it and spend time with it, you will find the emotion changes as you begin to process it.

In my mindfulness training, I learned that your suffering is the result of your actual pain multiplied by your resistance. As you let go of the resistance, you will feel your level of suffering diminish.

Working Through Challenging Emotions Exercise

This exercise is probably the biggest, most challenging, and potentially most transformational exercise of the entire book. It's a very deep exercise, so I recommend committing at least twenty minutes for this one. The idea is to bring to mind something you have resistance toward and practice exploring and making peace with the emotions that come up for you. By doing so, you will find that the emotions stop controlling you, and perhaps they have an insightful message for you.

If you have little energy or desire right now to bring up something activating, I recommend scheduling time in your calendar for this exercise within the next seven days.

Step 1: Make yourself comfortable and grounded. Then bring to mind something you have resistance toward and find upsetting or disappointing. Choose a situation that triggers you. You're looking for feelings of anger, fear, sadness, shame, or guilt.

If nothing springs to mind, sit quietly and ask yourself: *What am I not willing to feel? Which memory am I resisting? What am I most afraid of?* The answers to these questions will point you to the place you need to explore.

Step 2: Take a moment to recollect what the issue is all about and notice how you feel about it. For this exercise we want you to feel triggered or activated so you can go into the emotion and release it. Resist the temptation to stay in your head and analyze the back story. The purpose is to feel into the difficulty and release the tension at an emotional level, rather than thinking about it intellectually.

Step 3: Relax your body and acknowledge how you are feeling by naming your current emotions. *I feel vulnerable right now. Yes. And I feel really sad and alone right now. Yes.* Give yourself permission to simply name what is there without blaming anyone. You're not analyzing past scenarios in your mind and you're not trying to fix anything.

Step 4: Gently turn toward the emotion and with each in-breath say. *Allow. Allow. Allow.* Allow yourself to open up and get in touch with the emotional pain. With each out-breath say, *Soften. Soften. Soften.* Take slow, deep breaths and see if you can let go of tension each time you exhale. Simply sit, breathe, relax, and allow the emotions to be there.

Step 5: As an act of self-care, bring to mind something that helps you feel safe, loved, and grounded. This can be your circle of allies, feeling the support of your ancestors, putting a hand on your heart, or noticing your feet on the ground. It can also be helpful to say soothing phrases to yourself. You can try saying: *This is a challenging moment for me. That's okay. Everybody experiences challenging moments. I have the strength, support, and compassion I need to meet the situation.*

Step 6: If your emotional pain is still present, go deeper by identifying where in your body you are holding the tension. Where do you physically feel the emotion? Perhaps it's in your stomach, chest, shoulders, throat, or head? Be present with the sensations and breathe into them.

Step 7: Now, notice the shape, texture, and color of the emotion. Is it dense or is it moving? Does anything happen when you focus intensely on it?

Step 8: Finally, ask the emotion if it has a message for you. Be still and listen with your intuitive mind. What does the emotion need from you? What is it trying to make you realize?

Throughout this exercise, stay as curious and open as possible and embrace whatever comes up. There is no need to judge yourself. If you feel resistance to any of the steps, that's okay. Pause and notice it. See if you can relax a bit more. Remember you're not trying to actively get rid of the emotion. You're practicing accepting the emotion and opening up to it.

Emotional Freedom Technique

Emotional Freedom Technique (EFT), also known as tapping, is an evidence-based self-help method that can help you process and let go of difficult emotions. It was founded by Gary Craig in the early 1990's. It's similar to acupuncture in that it uses the meridian points of the body to restore balance. In essence, EFT works by gently tapping nine major meridian points on your face and body, one by one, as you keep in mind an unresolved emotional issue. Tapping on these points sends a calming signal to your amygdala. As you tap through the points, you repeat certain phrases to yourself that make the particular situation or emotion flare up. It may seem a bit strange at first, but you'll find that your mind and body naturally calm down as you tap through the points.

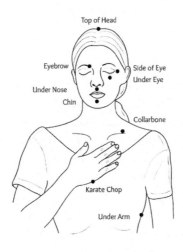

EFT Tapping Points

You can use this technique anytime you notice a strong emotional response in relation to a past memory, a situation in the present, or an imagined future event. You can also use it to overcome limiting beliefs and physical pain.

Let's say you feel upset because of an uncomfortable situation with another person. Perhaps you've had an argument with someone you care a great deal about and you feel they treated you unfairly. You might of course want to speak to the person about it directly, but as a first step it would be helpful to let go of the emotional charge so you can feel better and think more clearly when you communicate with them.

To start the EFT process, bring to mind the unpleasant situation and create your set-up statement. The set-up statement could be something to the effect of: *Even though I feel distressed and hurt by the actions of my friend, and it's so hard to let it go, I completely love and accept myself.* You are acknowledging the issue and how you're feeling and also adding a positive statement (I completely love and accept myself), thereby indicating that you're safe in spite of the issue.

The next step is to repeatedly tap on a particular point on the side of your hand, called the Karate Chop point, while repeating the set-up statement: *Even though I feel distressed and hurt by the actions of my friend, and it's so hard to let it go, I completely love and accept myself.* You repeat the sentence three times while continuously tapping the Karate Chop point with three or four fingers.

Next, tap the remaining eight meridian points starting at the top of your head and moving down your body while amplifying the storyline in your head and feeling all the emotions inside you. As you tap the various points you might say phrases like: *I feel so hurt by this dispute, it makes me sick to the stomach, I just can't believe it's got to that point, I feel so angry and frustrated, I know I'm carrying around this tension, and it's so hard to let go, I really don't know what to do, I'm unsure how to let it go, but I would really like to.*

Simply speak the words that come to you in the moment without overthinking them. Tell the story as you perceive it. Initially you might feel sad and agitated, but after a few rounds of tapping you will find that the emotions become less intense and your words become more open and positive. *I'm beginning to feel calmer now, I still feel a bit hurt, but I know I will be okay, I don't want this issue to keep affecting me, it's time to put it behind me, I think I'm ready to release it and let it go, right now.*

I personally got started with EFT by watching a tutorial on the internet and quickly got the hang of it. I was quite skeptical at first, but to my big surprise I felt emotionally cleansed after my first self-guided session. It was as if I'd had an internal shower. As I began to use the technique regularly, I relaxed into it and found it to be a valuable tool for processing and releasing my emotions.

When I use EFT, I often find that tears will flow when I start tapping and allow myself to feel the full force of my emotions. If I'm angry about something, I find that after a few rounds of tapping the anger will die down and be replaced by another emotion, perhaps sadness. It's fascinating to witness the emotions pass through me like weather systems passing through the sky. Fear, sadness, anger, laughter, and more sadness. But at the end I always feel calm. The emotions have been heard and they have run their course.

Expressive Writing

Another great method for processing difficult emotions is a technique described in David Hanscom's book, *Back in Control*.[70] Hanscom is a spine surgeon who suffered from anxiety and debilitating chronic back pain for decades. His misery started with an anxiety attack when driving across a bridge late one night. He had experienced anxiety his whole life but largely ignored it until his physical symptoms became so bad he could no longer ignore the pain. He was in a state of despair for years searching for something that could help. It wasn't until he began a regular practice of expressive writing that he rid himself of his emotional and physical distress. In fact, his pain and anxiety noticeably decreased within a couple of weeks. He then went on to help many of his patients recover without surgery by following his method.

Expressive writing is very simple. You spend about fifteen minutes in the morning and again at night writing down, preferably by hand, any positive or negative thoughts that come into your mind. You simply capture anything that comes up without analyzing or judging what you are writing. The purpose isn't to share or hold on to your notes afterwards so your writing doesn't need to make sense or even be legible. The point is simply to express your inner thoughts and feelings by writing them down.

After you've written out your thoughts in graphic and descriptive language, you immediately rip up the paper into small pieces and discard them. Tearing up the paper gives you freedom to write whatever is on your mind without fearing that anyone will read it afterwards. This method is very different than journaling because, with journaling, you hold on to the experiences you write about by going back and reading your words later.

It turns out that Hanscom initially stumbled upon expressive writing without knowing the method has been the subject of extensive studies. When Baikie and Wilhelm set out to review the research on expressive writing, they confirmed that people who write about stressful or emotional events benefit both physically and psychologically compared to those who write about neutral topics.[71]

There are different theories as to why expressive writing is so effective. Hanscom explains that the process creates awareness of your thoughts and separates you from them. By putting pen to paper, you become the observer of your thoughts and feelings, rather than identifying with them.[72] It's also thought that when you talk or write about something that disturbs you and acknowledge the associated emotions, the overall stress on the body is reduced because it lowers inhibition and ruminations.[73]

The techniques I have described above, which help you process and release pent up emotions, do come with a caveat. You need to be strong enough mentally and emotionally to sit with the emotions and tolerate them when they surface. If you feel too fragile at the moment to explore this on your own, I recommend you work with an experienced practitioner or a psychotherapist.

Expressive Writing Exercise

The goal of this exercise is to write about your stressful or emotional events for fifteen minutes. Doing so will reduce your overall stress and bring benefits to your physical and mental health. I recommend you use pen and paper rather than capturing your words electronically.

- Settle in a place where you feel safe and comfortable. To help you feel strong, bring to mind some of the resources you identified in Chapter 3. It doesn't matter if they are real or imagined as long as they have a positive effect on your psychology.
- Spend 15 minutes writing down anything that's on your mind. Don't think too much about it. Just write whatever comes up without pausing or analyzing. Simply dump all of your stresses and upsetting emotions on paper. Your handwriting does not need to be legible.
- After 15 minutes, stop and immediately tear up your paper without reading back your words.
- For maximum benefit, repeat this process twice a day.

How did you find this exercise? Do you feel lighter now after you purged your emotional stresses?

Embracing Emotions as They Appear

The first time you go into a strong emotion and sit with it, you might feel drained or you might find you're not able to fully complete the process. That's okay. There will be many opportunities to practice in day-to-day life. Whenever something triggers you, simply stop and name the feeling. Perhaps you feel angry that someone is cutting you off in traffic, you feel impatient standing in line, or you feel ignored by a boss or a loved one. When you notice that nagging gremlin at the door, surrender and turn toward it. *I'm feeling angry right now. Yes. I'm feeling not seen and not heard. Yes.* Simply acknowledging your feelings can sometimes be enough for them to flow through you and move on.

As you gradually bring your unwanted emotions into the light, you will begin to cycle through them quicker. It will feel less draining as you get better at handling the discomfort of your most intense emotions. Your challenging emotions won't vanish. Remember, the goal isn't to avoid or get rid of them. The goal is to create a relationship with your emotions where you regularly accept and acknowledge them. When you turn toward your unwanted emotions, they lose their power over you. This is an important step in healing. You have to bring those parts of you that were previously hidden into the light. When something is tucked away in your shadow it has the power to control you.

One of my coaching clients, Louise, used to feel incredibly angry to the point where the anger would consume her and trigger her to say and do things she would later regret. Her anger stemmed from the controlling force that church leaders had played in her life. She felt the church had stolen decades of her life by dictating how she lived until she sought help in her late 30's and began making her own choices in life. Her anger manifested as a red, hot fire in her throat and would easily flare up when she encountered certain people who represented the old-school thinking of the church.

For most of her life, she resisted the anger, hoping and wishing it would disappear on its own. But she built up her courage and finally faced it. For several weeks she would have a daily practice of sitting with the anger and letting it flare up. Then she would imagine cool blue water passing through her hot and angry throat until it extinguished the anger. This practice was transformational for her. The anger didn't go away, but it diminished dramatically. She learned how to be with it and listen to it instead of letting it consume her.

When you open up toward some of these unwanted parts of yourself, you will notice that your capacity to be with discomfort expands little by little. You will be able to tolerate a wider spectrum of emotions in yourself and in others, and it will become easier to embrace the messiness and ambiguity of life. That's liberating. This process will help you release tension and give you freedom to see things more clearly. You will no longer need to run away or fight what is happening. Instead, you'll find you can simply feel your feelings deeply and calmly choose how to respond.

Instead of seeking to change your outer environment to appease you, you will come to rely more on your inner resources. You will be more centered and less dependent on external circumstances for your emotional wellbeing. This kind of emotional maturity doesn't come overnight. It's a process, woven together by the many introspective moments and adjustments you make on a day-to-day basis.

As you make it a habit to use your emotional processing skills to handle the unavoidable chaos and challenging experiences in life, you will begin to shed old habits. You will no longer seek to control the uncontrollable. You will learn to accept the things you cannot change and find peace in doing so. You will realize that most of the stress and anxiety in your life came from your own bad habits of trying to avoid your feelings and change other people and circumstances. You will learn to make friends with your emotions and with uncertainty and discomfort, and you will find things that used to overwhelm you no longer bother you like they used to.

Dealing With Fear and Worry

There are all kinds of things you could worry about. Changes at the workplace, career development, your financial situation, your romantic relationship, your children's future, the natural word, society, your health, or the wellbeing of a loved one. These concerns are all reasonable. Your brain is wired to keep you and your loved ones safe and it's constantly scanning for threats in the environment. Some threats are worth listening to and acting on. However, many of our worries are blown out of proportion by an anxious mind and an overactive nervous system.

There will always be thoughts and intuitions we need to take seriously to prevent an issue from appearing further down the road. For instance, we all know we need to be proactive and take care of our heath to minimize the risk of illness. If we exercise, eat healthy foods, look after our emotional wellbeing, and get enough sleep, there is no need to worry. In fact, worrying is likely to erode our health. When we worry excessively, we trigger the sympathetic nervous system and reinforce the emotional experience of stress. Cortisol and adrenaline are released into the bloodstream, our focus narrows, and our immune system is suppressed so we can allocate more resources to fighting the perceived threat.

The only way out of fear is to go through it. Not to exacerbate it with intellectualizing and ruminating, but to be present with the emotion and challenge the thoughts behind it.

Whenever you feel overwhelmed due to high levels of change and uncertainty, breathe deeply from your abdomen and make your out-breaths longer than the in-breath. Then turn toward those uncomfortable emotions. Open the door and observe what is going on, even if it's uncomfortable. Where does the feeling of being overwhelmed sit in your body, and what does it need from you? Perhaps this is the scared part of you that needs comfort and compassion. Turn toward it, listen to it, and give it a hug. The emotion was kind enough to alarm you, so show it that you are okay and that you are safe. Reassure it that you have already taken action to protect yourself and your loved ones and that there is nothing more for you to do right now. All you need to do is relax and trust that everything will be all right.

At one point, I became consumed by fear and worry when I began to suffer from unexplained pain and neurological issues. For more than a year, I had felt burning and tingling sensations in both of my legs all the way from my lower back down to my heels. Initially I thought it would cure itself, but, as it became worse, I decided to consult my doctor. I took several blood tests, and I was referred to a neurologist, who arranged for a full MRI scan. All of these steps took time and left me in a state of uncertainly and worry for weeks. I began to search the internet and found that my symptoms could be a sign of anything from brain cancer and MS to permanent nerve damage. I felt overwhelmed with fear and anxiety about the future, and I knew I had to address it.

I decided to sit with my fear and really face it. I felt the fear fully in my body, I stayed with it, and I spoke to it. I surrendered and let myself be vulnerable. I was struggling, but my breath helped me stay present and experience what needed to be experienced. After I allowed myself to feel the fear to the point where it no longer consumed me, I had a closer look at the thoughts that were exacerbating my pain. Was it true that my life would be over if I was diagnosed with cancer or MS? No. Not necessarily. And how likely was it that I'd be diagnosed with something of that nature? Sure, there was a likelihood of bad news, but blood tests and physical examinations pointed toward something much less dramatic.

As I began to calm down and come back to my senses, my biology of courage started to emerge. I had strengthened the belief that I'd be able to handle it no matter what happened. I would have the resources inside me to deal with whatever life threw at me. With that attitude, fear had little place to spiral out of control because I had opened up to it, accepted it, and dialogued with it. This is not to say that sitting with my fear was a one-off exercise. Fear can be a frequent visitor because it's wired into our biology. I've become a lot better at noticing it, dialoguing with it, and stopping it from spiraling out of control.

The following week the results of the MRI scan came back and didn't show any sign of major pathology. I still had to get to the bottom of my issues, but the worst of my worries had turned out to just be worries, not real problems.

We've all had similar experiences. We go down a rabbit hole and are so identified with our thoughts and emotions that we don't see anything else. We become the emotion. We become the thought. We get consumed with worry, anxiety, or anger. Fortunately, we don't have to identify with our thoughts and emotions. With mindful awareness, we can take a step back, observe ourselves, dialogue with the emotion, and choose a different response. We can turn toward the unpleasant feelings and challenge our thought-patterns so that we can return to our center.

Shining the Light on Your Limiting Beliefs

In chapter 2 we touched upon some of the common thoughts and beliefs that can play havoc with your mind and with your emotions: *I'm not experienced enough, not clever enough, not kind enough, not slim enough. I'm too old, too young, too introverted.* The list goes on. Some of these beliefs are easy to identify because you perceive them as direct limitations.

Others may be harder to spot. You simply don't notice that they're a problematic part of your programming. For instance, *I can't relax and I can't be my true self when I'm with my boss. I have to say yes to every project I'm assigned or else I won't be seen as a valuable employee. I can't focus when it's noisy. Asking for help is a sign of weakness. I don't have enough money to follow my dreams.* When I first learned about limiting beliefs many years ago, I didn't think I had any. Ha! I later realized that I had many limiting beliefs that I had been blind to! They are a part of my programming.

What were the thoughts and beliefs behind my health anxiety? That I was broken and that my life as I knew it would be over. What were the beliefs behind Louise's anger? That the leaders of her church had restricted her choices in life and that she would not be able to regain what they took away.

Some years ago, I coached a young man called Dan, who was held back by his experiences and deeply ingrained limiting beliefs. When I first got to know him, he talked me through the past ten years of his life, and how he had gone from job to job and from woman to woman. Dan was intelligent and witty so it wasn't hard for him to charm a woman or land a new job whenever he wanted to. But Dan struggled to hold on to jobs and relationships. Each time, just when things were going well for him with a great new job and relationship, he would suddenly turn to gambling and stop turning up for work. What was going on? Why was he repeatedly sabotaging himself?

It turned out that Dan had experienced sexual abuse in his childhood and, in spite of several years of therapy, it was still having a major impact on him. His story made perfect sense, up until a point. He was the victim who hadn't yet healed his trauma, partly because he hadn't been ready to openly talk about it and process it.

As we continued our coaching sessions, something else emerged. Dan told me he felt he didn't deserve to stay in those good jobs he had and that he didn't deserve to be with those loving women because he was inherently a bad person. I said, "Dan, what happened to you in your childhood was not your fault. This was being done to you. You are not a bad person." Then he responded. "But Susanne, there is something I haven't told you. Back then in my childhood, when the sexual assault happened, I was not the victim. I was the perpetrator."

This opened up an entirely different conversation about how he'd been groomed through the internet and fallen victim to remote child abusers, who eventually influenced him to become a perpetrator himself. Dan was finally at a place where he could begin to admit what had happened and bring compassion and forgiveness to the situation. He had always seen himself as the perpetrator, but looking at it from an adult's point of view, it's easy to see that he was also the victim in many ways. There was still a long road of healing ahead of him, but he had taken the first important steps to healing by talking about what really happened, reflecting on his feelings, and taking a look at those experiences through a new perspective.

Now you may not relate to Dan's story of sexual abuse and perpetration, but all of us can relate to feelings and beliefs that hold us back from living the life we really want to live. If you feel insecure and inadequate because you believe you're not worthy of love or good things, then you will continue to self-sabotage just as Dan did. Maybe you self-sabotage by overeating, avoiding important conversations or tasks, or failing to speak up for yourself when you want or need something different than what you've been getting.

To dive deeply into your own limiting programming, ask yourself what the most difficult or painful thing is that you believe. Is there a thought or a story you are clinging to and contracting around? Chances are that deep down there is a limiting belief preventing you from moving forward. As you bring to mind this painful part of your life, notice what you are saying to yourself about the situation in your head. By observing your thoughts you gain insight into the limitations of your mind's programming.

Watch out for thoughts that seem to justify how you are feeling. For instance, *my family should be honest with me. I expect people to be on time.* These are examples of limiting thoughts that can cause a great deal of emotional stress. If you believe those thoughts, then you will believe you are justified in feeling those emotions. But it's actually believing and holding on to those thoughts that can cause you to feel angry, hurt, and afraid.

A powerful thought experiment is to imagine two different versions of yourself living in two parallel universes. In one universe you fully believe in your storyline and are the victim of your limiting beliefs. You keep yourself small and want to control the world around you because you've given in to your doubt and fear. In the other universe you're living a completely different life because you've let go of your limiting beliefs. Can you see the dramatic difference? Can you imagine who you would be without giving in to these limiting thoughts and beliefs?

A helpful tool to deconstruct your thinking is to separate your beliefs from the actual facts of the situation. Instead of telling yourself the story that you're a failure or a nobody, stick with observable facts: *I've lost my job. Or my bosses don't say good morning to me.*[74] Stories and beliefs are interpretations of observations. They can easily limit you and make you feel like a victim. Facts are easier to do something about. By deconstructing your thinking, you give yourself the chance to actively choose how to interpret a certain event. For example, *I've lost my job. I feel angry and terrified. But I won't let this break me. I choose to see it as an opportunity to find a role that is better suited to my strengths and values.*

As you begin to observe and challenge your thoughts, you may come to see that some of your stories were helpful defense mechanisms in the past. There is no need to blame yourself for that. Simply becoming aware of your limiting thoughts can set you free. Joseph Goldstein says that thoughts are like little dictators of the mind. *Go here! Go there! Do this! Do that!* And we just follow along, pushed by our thoughts. He explains that thoughts have tremendous power, but when you're aware of thoughts they have no power at all except for the thoughts you choose to believe or act on.[75]

As soon as you become aware of a thought-pattern that is not serving you, you have the power to control it and change it. But the thoughts you aren't conscious of are in control of you. The more curious you become, the more you will become aware that your thoughts don't define you. They are not who you are. You can separate yourself from them. You can observe them. You can question them. You can let go of them and you can deliberately choose a better thought. That's how you free yourself from limiting beliefs. When a limiting thought arises, ask yourself if this is really who you are or if it's just an experience that is moving through you.

With the knowledge that you are not your thoughts, you can actively step away from thoughts that are harmful and cultivate and act upon those that serve you and your community. This is not a shift that happens overnight, but with conscious effort and a healthy dose of self-compassion you can change your life quicker than you think. If your old programming pops up again, or you have a destructive thought, notice that you're having the unhelpful thought, forgive yourself, and let the thought pass. Then choose a different thought that is more aligned with who you want to be.

The real route to freedom and feeling centered and at peace is to cultivate awareness. When you are aware of your thoughts and emotions you can take a step back and avoid getting consumed by them. When you can observe your thoughts and emotions with openness and curiosity you're no longer being blindly controlled by your unconscious programming. You're fully awake and able to choose how to respond to the curveballs life throws at you. De Mello writes that the only way to awareness is to watch yourself with no interference or judgment on your part. He recommends not to personalize what is happening to you, but to simply watch yourself as if you were looking at someone else. Then you will make great discoveries. And these discoveries will change you, he writes.[76]

Whenever you're in conversation with someone, observe your mind with a curious and objective attitude. If you notice you're getting triggered by what they're saying or doing, make an effort to breathe deeply and relax your body. This will help you generate awareness, let go of tension, and avoid being hijacked by your emotions. The beauty of the breath is that it will bring you right back to your senses and to the present moment when you focus on it. You can stop yourself from going into an automatic fight-or-flight reaction and instead consciously choose an appropriate response. Later, when you have time, you can go back to the situation and feel those feelings again to better process and understand them.

Change Your Story Exercise

Well done for having come this far! You have reached the last exercise on your journey of growth and self-discovery. And it's a very important exercise because it will help you become aware of the thoughts that cause you to feel anxious, unhappy, or emotionally off center. With that awareness, you can begin to question your thoughts and choose more empowering ones. Set aside at least ten minutes for this exercise.

Step 1: Think about an area of your life where you are holding yourself back or feel anxious or unhappy about your lack of progress. Perhaps you're unhappy about your body, you worry about your finances, you feel anxious about the state of the world, or you find it hard to relax.

Step 2: As you bring to mind this painful aspect of your life, notice how you talk to yourself about it in your head. What are you saying to yourself? Is there a thought or storyline you are clinging to and contracting around? Are you telling yourself that you are flawed in some way, that there isn't enough time or money, or that something needs to happen in order for you to make progress and feel at ease now? See if you can uncover the conditions and limitations of the way you think about this situation.

Step 3: Notice who inside of you is telling the story. Is it your wise higher self or is it the small victim you, who likes to place blame or justify the situation?

Step 4: Notice if there is an element of fear in the story. For instance, *it's better to stay in my current situation even if it's unfulfilling because I could end up worse off if I make a change.*

Step 5: Now, relax your abdomen and breathe slowly. Then take the position of a neutral observer. Imagine floating out of your body and looking down on yourself from above. What do you notice when you look at yourself from the outside? Can you see that your story is one-sided and it's not the full truth?

Step 6: How could you rewrite your story and make it more empowering? Which new beliefs do you need to incorporate into your thinking in order to feel better about your situation? You can try thoughts like: *I have the strength inside of me to move forward in spite of the uncertainty of the future. When I focus on the peacefulness of my heart, I'm able to relax even if everything in my life is far from perfect. Even if I say no to this assignment, I know that I am worthy of love.* Identify at least two new empowering beliefs and write them down.

What did you learn from this exercise? Are you able to see that your emotional state is dictated by your level of thinking and that by changing your limiting beliefs you are able to come home to yourself right this moment?

Change Your Expectations for Appreciation

When you observe yourself and cultivate awareness, you become more conscious of your attachments and how much your happiness depends on them. For instance, *when I get more time, I'll be able to relax. When my relationship settles, I'll be happy. When I finally lose weight, I'll feel at ease. When I get that new job, I'll be sure of myself.* As you observe yourself and unravel the stories your mind is holding on to, you will get a glimpse of the many ways in which you are keeping yourself from being centered and relaxed. The stories you're telling yourself are giving you reasons why you cannot be at peace now.

In his book, *A New Earth*, Eckhart Tolle writes, "The primary cause of unhappiness is never the situation but your thoughts about it... The ego says maybe at some point in the future I can be at peace if this, that, or the other happens."[77] When we focus on what we don't have, we take away our peace. Therefore, the question we need to ask ourselves is: What needs to happen in order for me to be at peace right now? Chances are, we would all be more peaceful if we were to drop some of our desires and expectations and just accept the way things are in this present moment.

As long as your expectations are out of sync with reality, you will continue to feel unhappy, tense, and stressed. Tony Robbins says that to be fulfilled you must change your expectations for appreciation. If you get too caught up in what you expect and feel entitled to something, you will likely set yourself up for disappointment. That doesn't mean you shouldn't have hopes and wishes for the future. Having the desire to live a meaningful life in alignment with your values is a good thing. It just means that it's unwise to be too attached to your desires. You will feel more at peace if you accept the reality of any given moment.

When my physical pain was at its highest, I suffered from insomnia and could barely sit or walk because of the pain and inflammation in my joints. I felt plagued with feelings of sadness and hopelessness. I knew I had to accept my current reality while working toward a brighter future. I had many days where I felt depressed and victimized. I continued to work on my mindset, cultivate compassion for myself, and build a new empowering narrative. My narrative was: *No matter what caused me to feel this way, my mind and body has the power to heal itself.* I also told myself that there was a higher purpose in going through this, and that, at the end of the day, I would come out the other end as a healthier, wiser, and more compassionate person. Telling myself this empowering story helped me relax, trust that everything would be okay, and allow my nervous system to calm down and support my healing.

My wish for you is that you keep taking conscious action so you can live a fulfilled and purposeful life. But don't let it crush you if the universe throws you a curveball. Life is joyful and painful and everything in between. We all need some adversity to grow and progress. The sooner you accept that, and the sooner you relax your expectations, the freer you will be. To quote Shakespeare, "For there is nothing either good or bad, but thinking makes it so."[78]

Practicing being okay with whatever is going on around you is one of the keys to peace and happiness. That's not an easy thing to do. You may have spent a lifetime building your identity, accumulating material possessions, and viewing the world through the lens of your programming. But if you are too attached to your identity, your job, your daily routine, your health, and to other people behaving in a certain way, it will lead to greater suffering when your needs and desires aren't met. In fact, too much attachment can lead to anxiety. You begin to fear that things won't go as you expect, or that you may lose something which you treasure. The more attached you are, the more fearful and unhappy you may become.

Ironically, we live in an increasingly uncertain, complex, and unstable world. Society changes all the time, organizations change, family structures change, technology changes, the climate changes and the world-order changes. In such a world, where change is happening at a faster and faster rate, you do need something to hold on to. But instead of clinging to external events and physical things, let that something be your own inner resources and the strength of your spirit.

Hold on to that deep sense of peace that comes when you close your eyes, fully relax your body and mind, and focus on your heart space. Take a deep, slow breath and use it to come back to your senses. Bring forth any images, words, sounds, sensations, movements, or experiences that make you feel safe and at ease. Put a hand on your heart, breathe out slowly, and notice your feet against the ground. Imagine your circle of allies and say soothing phrases to yourself. *I feel safe. I know I'm able to handle this. I will always be here for you. I love you no matter what.*

Hold on to the belief that no matter what happens you will be able to deal with it. When you expand into the safe and loving space that already exists within you, you will be able to face the uncertainty outside of you. You are already standing on a mountain full of experiences, strengths, attributes, and support. In fact, you are that mountain. Calm and steady. Strong and grounded. The storm and the rain can't tear you down. They merely touch your surface as they move across the sky and make way for the sun.

References

Books

Amy B. Scher, *How to Heal Yourself When No One Else Can.* Llewellyn Publications, 2019

Anthony De Mello, *Awareness.* Fount Paperbacks, 1997

Bruce Lipton, The Biology of Belief: Unleashing the power of consciousness, matter and miracles. Cygnus Books, 2005

Charlie Morley, *Wake Up to Sleep*: 5 Powerful practices to transform stress & trauma for peaceful sleep & mindful dreams. Hay House, 2021

Choden & Heather Regan-Addis, *Mindfulness Based Living Course.* O-Books, 2018

Dan Brulé, *Just Breathe: Mastering Breathwork.* Enliven Books/Atria Paperback, 2017

David Hanscom, *Back in Control: A surgeon's roadmap out of chronic pain.* Vertus Press (2nd ed.), 2016

Eckhart Tolle, *A New Earth: Crate a better life.* Penguin Books, 2016

James Nestor, *Breath: The New Science of a Lost Art.* PENGUIN LIFE, 2021

Mark Wolynn, *It Didn't Start With You: How Inherited Family Trauma Shapes Who We Are and How to End the Cycle.* Penguin Books, 2017

Michael A. Singer, *The Untethered Soul: The Journey Beyond Yourself.* New Harbinger Publications, 2007

Osho, Meditation for busy people: Stress-beating strategies to calm your life. Hamlyn, 2004

The Sivananda Yoga Center, *Sivananda Beginner's Guide to Yoga.* Gaia, 2006

Websites

Sounds True
www.resources.soundstrue.com

The Mindfulness Association
www.mindfulnessassociation.net

Huberman Lab
www.hubermanlab.com

NeuroDynamic Breathwork™
www.breathworkonline.com

Alchemy of Breath
www.alchemyofbreath.com

Tara Brach
www.tarabrach.com

Dr. Kristin Neff. Self-Compassion Test
www.self-compassion.org/self-compassion-test

Center for Healthy Minds
www.centerhealthyminds.org

HeartMath Institute
www.heartmath.org

For more links, visit:
www.susannemadsen.co.uk/inner-work.html

Acknowledgements

I would like to thank my friends and family for their ongoing love and support. I would also like to thank everyone who provided their honest feedback and encouragement on earlier versions of this book, including Annette Simmons, Tom Corson-Knowles, Sharon K. Summerfield, Ruth Pearce, Tatyana Sussex, Adrian, Sandra, and Nina.

On my path to coming home to myself, I owe a lot to Elizabeth Luminati for helping me understand and process my emotions, when I came to her for psychotherapy many years ago.

I'm also deeply appreciative of my many coaching clients from whom I have learned so much, as well as the many teachers and mentors whose wisdom I continue to draw inspiration from, including Andrew Huberman, Anthony De Mello, Bruce Lipton, Caroline Myss, Deepak Chopra, Eckhart Tolle, Jack Kornfield, Gabor Maté, Lars Muhl, Marianne Williamson, Michael Singer, Osho, Tara Brach, Tami Simon, Tony Robbins, and many more—as well as Choden and all the teachers at the Mindfulness Association.

Thank you, thank you, thank you!

About the Author

Susanne Madsen is an internationally recognized executive coach, speaker, and award-winning author of *The Power of Project Leadership*. She is known for her transformational leadership programs and has coached hundreds of individuals from high-profile organizations across the globe. A leading voice in the field of leadership and personal development, Susanne helps her clients free themselves from the limitations of their thoughts and minds and live truly fulfilling lives.

Other Books by Susanne Madsen

The Power of Project Leadership: *7 Keys to Help you Transform from Project Manager to Project Leader: 2nd edition. Kogan Page, 2019. (Also translated to Polish and Mandarin)*

The Project Management Coaching Workbook: *Six Steps to Unleashing Your Potential, Berrett-Koehler Publishers, 2012*

Connect With Susanne Madsen

To find out more information visit her website:
www.susannemadsen.com

To access selected exercises from this book as
audio recordings visit:
www.susannemadsen.co.uk/inner-work.html

Social media links:

www.linkedin.com/in/susanne-madsen-1134312

www.youtube.com/susannemadsen

www.twitter.com/SusanneMadsen

www.tiktok.com/@susannemadsenint

Book Discounts and Special Deals

Sign up for free to get discounts and special deals
on our bestselling books at
www.TCKpublishing.com/bookdeals

Endnotes

1   We know from Shawn Achor's research and TED talk that our wellbeing is only 10% determined by external circumstances such as education, demographics and genetics. 90% of long-term happiness (and wellbeing) can be predicted, not based on external circumstances but on how our brain processes those circumstances. *How happiness affects your success: Interview with Shawn Achor.* SpeakersOffice. 2014, September 9. Retrieved October 11, 2023, from https://www.speak-ersoffice.com/happiness-affects-success-interview-shawn-achor/

2   Myss, C. & Shealy, N. (2023, February). *The Science of Medical Intuition. Sounds True Online Course.*

3   Lipton, B. H. (2005). *The Biology of Belief.* Cygnus Books.

4   Neff, K. (2013). *Self-Compassion: The proven power of being kind to yourself.* William Morrow Paperbacks, 2015, (https://www.goodreads.com/work/quotes/15024831-self-compassion-stop-beating-yourself-up-and-leave-insecurity-behind?page=2)

5   Neff, K. (2015, September). *The five myths of self-compassion.* Greater Good Magazine. Retrieved October 11, 2023, from https://greatergood.berkeley.edu/article/item/the_five_myths_of_self_compassion

6   Whole.TV. (2020). *Exhausted. Episode 9.*

7   If you would like to learn more about this way of giving feedback, look up *Nonviolent Communication* by Marshall B. Rosenberg. https://www.cnvc.org/learn/what-is-nvc

8   University of Minnesota. *Why is life purpose important?* Taking Charge of Your Health & Wellbeing. Retrieved October 11, 2023, from https://www.takingcharge.csh.umn.edu/why-life-purpose-important

9   Whole.TV. (2020). *Exhausted. Episode 9.*

10   Gandhi, M. *Be the change you wish to see in the world.* Quote Investigator. Retrieved October 11, 2023, from https://quoteinvesti-

gator.com/2017/10/23/be-change/#f+17089+1+2

11   Kornfield, J. (2020, July) *Love in action: Joining Together to Create a More Caring, Equitable, and Joyful World.* Sounds True Foundation. Retrieved October 11, 2023, from https://soundstruefoundation.org/love-in-action-webinar/?fbclid=IwAR0IvWo5BPgVa972E_Zg-PUj6IOCQJrm9UJUIHdFgVgut7VD_tnZnNppujFg

12   De Mello, A. (1997). *Awareness.* Fount (Reissue).

13   Steiner, S. (2012, February). *Top Five regrets of the dying.* The Guardian. Retrieved October 11, 2023, from https://www.theguardian.com/lifeandstyle/2012/feb/01/top-five-regrets-of-the-dying

14   Williamson, M. (1996). *A Return to Love: Reflections on the Principles of a Course in Miracles.* HarperOne.

15   Brulé, D. (2017). *Just breathe: Mastering breathwork.* Enliven Books/Atria Paperback.

16   Perry, P. (2017, January). *How we breathe affects our thoughts and emotions, northwestern researchers find.* Big Think. Retrieved October 11, 2023, from https://bigthink.com/neuropsych/how-we-breathe-effects-our-thoughts-and-feelings-northwestern-neuroscientists-find/

17   Brulé, D. (2017). *Just breathe: Mastering breathwork.* Enliven Books/Atria Paperback.

18   Garbing, P. *Michael Dresser Interviews Dr. Gerbarg about The Healing Power of the Breath.* Breath-Body-Mind. Retrieved October 11, 2023, from https://www.breath-body-mind.com/healing-power-of-the-breath

19   Lipton, B. (2023, February). *Trauma super conference.* Conscious Life. Retrieved February 18, 2023, from https://www.consciouslife.com/conferences/tsc-3/agenda

20   Lipton, B. (2019, August 26). *Bruce Lipton explains how thoughts cause illness and disease in the body.* Fearless Motivation. Retrieved October 11, 2023, from https://www.fearlessmotivation.com/2019/08/26/bruce-lipton-explains-how-thoughts-cause-disease-in-the-body/

21   Komori, T. (2018, May). The relaxation effect of prolonged expiratory breathing. Mental illness. Retrieved October 11, 2023, from https://www.ncbi.nlm.nih.gov/pmc/articles/PMC6037091/

22   Other ways to stimulate the parasympathetic nervous system are to spend time in nature, laughing, singing, dancing, playing with animals or children, exercising with moderation, getting a massage, and meditating.

23   Strom, M. (2015, December). *Breathe to heal | Max Strom | tedxcapemay*. YouTube. Retrieved October 11, 2023, from https://www.youtube.com/watch?v=4Lb5L-VEm34

24   Brulé, D. (2017). *Just breathe: Mastering breathwork*. Enliven Books/Atria Paperback.

25   Huberman, A. (2021, October). *Breathing techniques to reduce stress and anxiety | Dr. Andrew Huberman on the physiological sigh*. YouTube. Retrieved October 11, 2023, from https://www.youtube.com/watch?v=kSZKIupBUuc

26   Joseph, C. N., et al. (2005). Slow breathing improves arterial baroreflex sensitivity and decreases blood pressure in essential hypertension. *Hypertension*, *46*(4), https://www.ahajournals.org/doi/full/10.1161/01.hyp.0000179581.68566.7d

27   Busch, V., et al. (2012, February). The effect of deep and slow breathing on pain perception, autonomic activity, and mood processing—an experimental study. *Pain Medicine*, *13*(2), https://doi.org/10.1111/j.1526-4637.2011.01243.x

28   Ma, X., et al. (2017). The effect of diaphragmatic breathing on attention, negative affect and stress in healthy adults. *Frontiers in Psychology*, *8*. https://www.ncbi.nlm.nih.gov/pmc/articles/PMC5455070/

29   NESTOR, J. (2021). *Breath: The new science of a lost art*. PENGUIN LIFE.

30   NESTOR, J. (2021). *Breath: The new science of a lost art*. PENGUIN LIFE.

31   The Sivananda Yoga Centre. (2006). *Sivananda Beginner's guide to yoga*. Gaia.

32   Perry, P. (2017, January 19). *Déjà vu is a neurological phenomenon, scientists claim*. Big Think. Retrieved October 11, 2023, from https://bigthink.com/culture-religion/deja-vu-is-a-neurological-phenomenon-scientists-claim/

33   Gross, T. (2020, May 27). How the "lost art" of breathing can impact sleep and resilience. NPR. Retrieved October 11, 2003, from https://www.npr.org/sections/health-shots/2020/05/27/862963172/how-the-lost-art-of-breathing-can-impact-sleep-and-resilience

34   YouTube. (2019, November). *Coherent breathing's iconic 2 bells now with sinusoidal pacing. breathing exercises, breathwork*. YouTube. Retrieved February 18, 2023, from https://www.youtube.com/watch?v=E2qCSu75cOk&t=43s

35   Stančák, A., & Kuna, M. (1994). EEG changes during forced alternate nostril breathing. *International Journal of Psychophysiology, 18*(1), 75–79. https://www.sciencedirect.com/science/article/abs/pii/0167876084900175

36   Telles, S., et al (2017). Alternate-nostril yoga breathing reduced blood pressure while increasing performance in a vigilance test. *Medical Science Monitor Basic Research, 23*, https://www.ncbi.nlm.nih.gov/pmc/articles/PMC5755948/

37   (2015, April 9). *Yogis ahead of science: One nostril breathing determines how you feel*. The Yoga Space. Retrieved October 11, 2023, from https://theyogaspace.co.uk/yogis-ahead-of-science-one-nostril-breathing-determines-how-you-feel/

38   Nestor, J. (2021). *Breath: The new science of a lost art*. PENGUIN LIFE.

39   Brulé, D. (2017). *Just breathe: Mastering breathwork*. Enliven Books/Atria Paperback.

40   Look up https://breathworkonline.com for more information. https://alchemyofbreath.com runs similar sessions.

41   *Chasing the Present.* (2020). Documentary by Mark Waters. (Seen at the Hay House Summit).

42   Tolle, E. (2016). *A New Earth: Crate a Better Life.* Penguin Books.

43   Tolle, E. (2016). *A New Earth: Crate a Better Life.* Penguin Books.

44   Osho. (2004). *Meditation for busy people: Stress-beating strategies to calm your life.* Hamlyn.

45   Chopra, D. (2018, March). *7 ways meditation can help you reduce and manage stress.* Chopra. Retrieved October 11, 2023, from https://chopra.com/articles/7-ways-meditation-can-help-you-reduce-and-manage-stress?utm_source=Newsletter&utm_medium=Email&utm_content=200303-March-Newsletter&utm_campaign=Newsletter202033

46   McGreevey, S. (2011, January). *Eight Weeks to a better brain.* Harvard Gazette. Retrieved October 11, 2023, from https://news.harvard.edu/gazette/story/2011/01/eight-weeks-to-a-better-brain/

47   Janssen, M., et al. (2018). Effects of mindfulness-based stress reduction on employees' Mental Health: A Systematic Review. *PLOS ONE, 13*(1). https://journals.plos.org/plosone/article?id=10.1371/journal.pone.0191332

48   Chalmers, R. (2019, July). *Summary of Scientific Research on the Transcendental Meditation and TM-Sidhi Program.* Official Transcendental Meditation® Website. Retrieved October 11, 2023, from https://uk.tm.org/documents/12132/0/TM+Research+Summary+-+Chalmers+16+September+2017.pdf

49   Scott, E. (2022, September 22). *Transcendental Meditation and Its Many Benefits.* Verywell Mind. Retrieved October 11, 2023, from https://www.verywellmind.com/transcendental-meditation-and-its-many-benefits-4159899

50   Osho. (2004). *Meditation for busy people: Stress-beating strategies to calm your life.* Hamlyn.

51   Osho. (2004). *Meditation for busy people: Stress-beating strategies to calm your life*. Hamlyn.

52   *The Science of HeartMath*. HeartMath. Retrieved October 11, 2023, from https://www.heartmath.org/science/

53   Braden, G. (2021, February). *Hay House HEAL Summit 2021*. Hay House.

54   *Exploring the Role of the Heart in Human Performance, An Overview of Research Conducted by the HeartMath Institute*. Retrieved October 11, 2023, from https://www.heartmath.org/research/science-of-the-heart/energetic-communication/

55   *The Science of HeartMath*. HeartMath. Retrieved October 11, 2023, from https://www.heartmath.org/science/

56   *The Science of HeartMath*. HeartMath. Retrieved October 11, 2023, from https://www.heartmath.org/research/science-of-the-heart/energetic-communication/

57   Mickey Lemle. (2017). *The Last Dalai Lama?* Documentary.

58   Dr. Dr. Joe Dispenza is a researcher, lecturer and author in the field of mind-body medicine. Dispenza , J. (2016, November). *The Power of Gratitude*. Unlimited with Dr. Dr. Joe Dispenza. Retrieved October 11, 2023, from https://drjoedispenza.com/blogs/dr-joes-blog/the-power-of-gratitude

59   *The Science of Gratitude & How to Build a Gratitude Practice | Huberman Lab Podcast #47*. (2021, November). *YouTube*. Retrieved October 11, 2023, from https://www.youtube.com/watch?v=KVjfF-N89qvQ

60   Ilibagiza, I., & Erwin, S. (2014). *Left to tell: One Woman's Story of Surviving the Rwandan Holocaust*. Hay House.

61   Tony Robbins Foundation. (2009). *"Strangers care" Thanksgiving (Tony Robbins)*. YouTube. Retrieved October 11, 2023, from https://www.youtube.com/watch?v=CSM3Uml4Xpo

62   *Mission and history*. The Tony Robbins Foundation. Retrieved

October 11, 2023, from https://www.thetonyrobbinsfoundation.org/about-us/

63   Wilson, A. (2019, October 9). *The evidence-based benefits of loving-kindness meditation*. Kripalu. Retrieved October 11, 2023, from https://kripalu.org/resources/evidence-based-benefits-loving-kind-ness-meditation

64   Lutz, A., Brefczynski-Lewis, J., Johnstone, T., & Davidson, R. J. (2008). Regulation of the neural circuitry of emotion by Compassion Meditation: Effects of meditative expertise. *PLoS ONE, 3*(3). https://journals.plos.org/plosone/article?id=10.1371/journal.pone.0001897

65   Mickey Lemle. (2017). *The Last Dalai Lama?* Documentary.

66   *How mindfulness changes the emotional life of our brains | Richard J. Davidson | TEDxSanFrancisco*. (2019). *TED Talk*. Retrieved October 11, 2023, from https://www.ted.com/talks/richard_j_david-son_how_mindfulness_changes_the_emotional_life_of_our_brains_jan_2019?language=en.

67   Mickey Lemle. (2017). *The Last Dalai Lama?* Documentary.

68   Goldstein, J. *Joseph Goldstein on Knowing Mindfulness, PART 1 TALK: Mindfulness of Thoughts*. Dr. Rick Hanson. Retrieved October 11, 2023, from https://www.rickhanson.net/lkg-day-three/

69   Annette Simmons is a leadership coach and author of *Quantum Skills for coaches: A handbook for working with energy and the body-mind in coaching*. HotHive Books. (2008)

70   Hanscom, D. (2017). *Back in control: A Surgeon's roadmap out of chronic pain* (2nd ed.). Vertus Press.

71   Baikie, K. A., & Wilhelm, K. (2018). Emotional and physical health benefits of expressive writing. *Cambridge University Press, 11*(5), 338–346. https://doi.org/10.1192/apt.11.5.338

72   Hanscom, D. (2018). *Expressive writing: Your first step to eliminate chronic pain*. Retrieved October 11, 2023, from https://www.osteopath-hannover.com/wp-content/uploads/Expressive-Writing-v2.pdf

73   Baikie, K. A., & Wilhelm, K. (2018). Emotional and physical health benefits of expressive writing. *Cambridge University Press*, *11*(5), 338–346. https://doi.org/10.1192/apt.11.5.338

74   Tolle, E. (2016). *A New Earth: Create a Better Life*. Penguin Books.

75   Goldstein, J. *Joseph Goldstein on Knowing Mindfulness, PART 1 TALK: Mindfulness of Thoughts*. Dr. Rick Hanson. Retrieved October 11, 2023, from https://www.rickhanson.net/lkg-day-three/

76   De Mello, A. (1997). *Awareness*. Fount (Reissue).

77   Tolle, E. (2016). *A New Earth: Create a Better Life*. Penguin Books.

78   William Shakespeare's tragedy, Hamlet. It appears in Act II, Scene 2 and is spoken by Hamlet.

Printed in Great Britain
by Amazon